Earth Energies

Earth Energies

By the Editors of Time-Life Books

TIME-LIFE BOOKS, ALEXANDRIA, VIRGINIA

CONTENTS

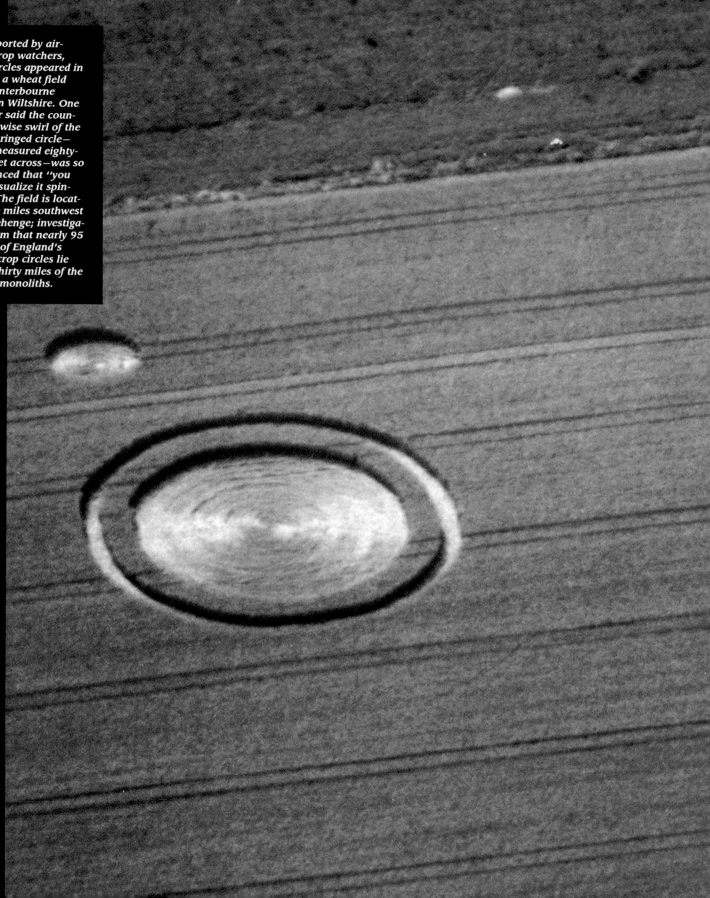

First reported by airborne crop watchers, these circles appeared in 1987 in a wheat field near Winterbourne Stoke, in Wiltshire. One observer said the counterclockwise swirl of the largest, ringed circle—which measured eighty-three feet across—was so pronounced that "you could visualize it spinning." The field is located three miles southwest of Stonehenge; investigators claim that nearly 95 percent of England's known crop circles lie within thirty miles of the ancient monoliths.

Curious Circles in the Grain

Upon first seeing the strange crop circles, one pilot said he nearly fell out of his plane. The circles became the most puzzling phenomenon of the era, appearing literally overnight throughout the world and proliferating almost exponentially: two or three a year in the 1970s, growing to 750 by the end of 1990, five hundred of them in that year alone.

Within the circles, flattened grain plants remained alive and unbroken—as if the stalks were softened, bent to the ground in swirling patterns, then rehardened. Many have been surrounded by concentric rings or have been part of increasingly intricate designs. Investigators have pondered myriad theoretical causes *(page 20)*—from herds of crazed hedgehogs trampling in circles to UFOs touching down unobserved. A few crop circles have proved to be hoaxes. But most, including these photographed in the southern English counties of Hampshire and Wiltshire, have seemed a mute, living testimony to what we have yet to learn about our planet and its sometimes mysterious energies. The tramline-like tracks in the pictures are tractor paths made by farmers.

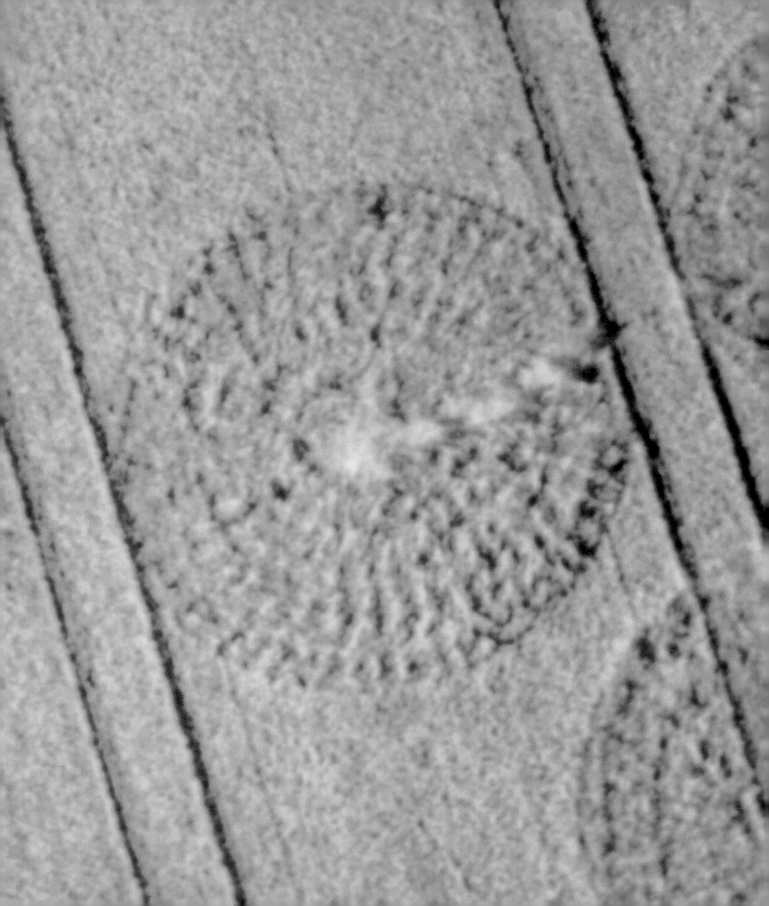

This triad of crop circles was found at southern Hampshire's Corhampton Downs farm in 1988—the third time in four years that circles had appeared on the farm. Repeat occurrences are not unusual, but the circles rarely form in exactly the same configurations each time. In this instance, the barley within each circle was flattened into patterns of seven concentric rings; then certain plants apparently righted themselves, forming forty-eight spokes radiating from the circle's center.

These five symmetrically placed circles appeared in 1987 near the village of Upton Scudamore in Wiltshire. Of particular note to one crop circle investigator was the unusually high incidence of UFO sightings reported near the village. It has been suggested that this cluster could be the imprint of an alien spaceship come to earth, with the largest circle representing the body of the craft and the four smaller circles its landing gear.

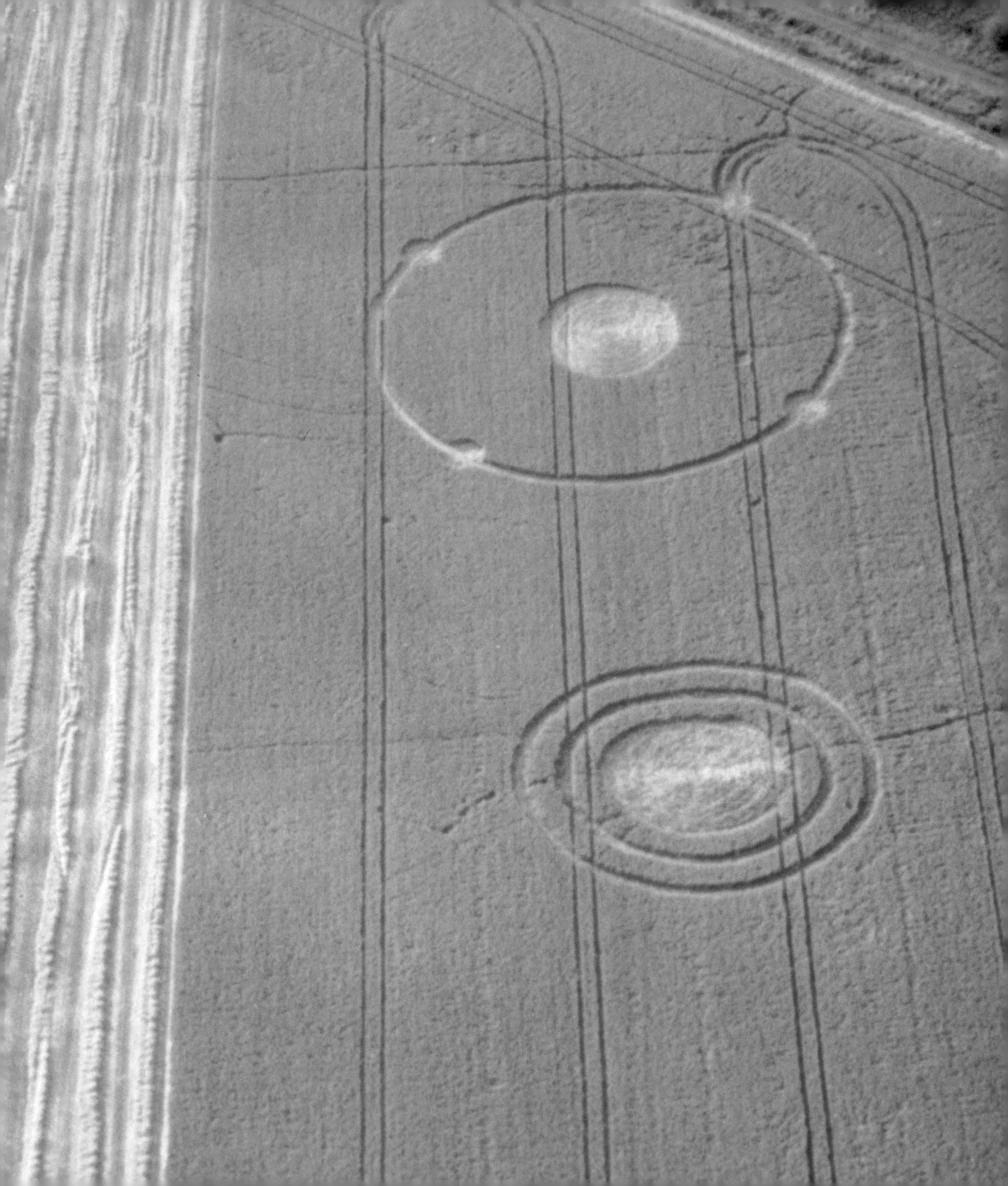

In 1988, a farmer harvesting his wheat near Clatford, Hampshire, discovered the two ringed circles pictured here. The farmer, whose handiwork is apparent in the denuded section of field at the left of the photograph, invited crop circle researchers to take a look before he destroyed the evidence. Some observers have suggested that the circle at top, surrounded by one ring that is intersected by four smaller circles, resembles the shape of a traditional Celtic cross.

Sightseers roam the elaborate Alton Barnes crop circle chain, which extended 510 feet through a Wiltshire field. The chain materialized in July 1990, marking the first time rectangles had appeared in a crop pattern. A week after the Alton Barnes discovery, another pattern of lines and circles appeared some fifteen miles away. But exultant observers were chagrined to find these crops had been trampled by hoaxers who had used—then left behind—a horoscope board game to design the pattern.

The Earth's Elusive Spirit

Judging by the tumbled and half-buried remains of crude stone houses discovered in the part of Northern Ireland that was once called County Tyrone, Neolithic farmers from the mainland of Europe probably settled in Ireland as long ago as 4700 BC. Within a thousand years they were erecting shrines to their deities and raising massive earthwork burial mounds. And by approximately 3500 BC, they had succeeded in building a masterpiece—a complex of extraordinary multichambered funerary mounds at Bend on the Boyne, not far from the city of Drogheda in Eire. There, along a wide curve of the river, three immense man-made hillocks command a view of the valley that surrounds them. Their domain is strewn with other, smaller barrows, as well as numerous standing stones, called menhirs, and circles of ancient megaliths—all of them testimony to the valley's long history as a sacred ground.

The greatest of the monuments is the mound called Newgrange, which has been compared to the ruins at Stonehenge because of the profound reaction it elicits from visitors. Many first-time observers are struck by the shape of the monument, which is queerly modern looking for such an archaic structure; some visitors even say that it bears an uncanny resemblance to a flying saucer. The stone face of one side of the mound has been fully restored in recent years; it gleams with bright white quartz and shines from a distance, looking as if it might be the body of a spacecraft. Above this wall, the gently rounded, grassy top of the hill completes the UFO illusion. A small doorway located at the center of the wall gives entrance to a narrow, sixty-two-foot-long passage, which leads to a large interior chamber that is topped by a corbeled stone ceiling. Three smaller rooms surround the main chamber. Above the entrance to the mound, a second, smaller opening that is shaped like a transom window admits light to the outer end of the passageway.

So old are the ruins at Newgrange that precise details of the religious or ceremonial practices that once were carried out there are well-nigh impossible to discover. Archaeologists agree, however, that the mound was almost certainly a bustle of activity during the winter solstice. For on that day, precisely at dawn, the rays of the rising sun align to penetrate the entire length of the passageway and illuminate the rear wall of the great chamber. There, they fall upon stone that is covered with distinctive spiral-shaped carvings. These symbols—in addition to being lovely to look at—have attracted the attention of anthropologists as well as historians because of their appearance in many other megalithic sites across the north of Europe and from Spain in the south to Scotland. The exact meaning of the spirals has proved difficult to determine, but the carvings seem to be associated with the cult of the Great Mother, or Mother Goddess. This archetypal figure of myth has turned up in one form or another in virtually every primitive culture throughout the world. The goddess is celebrated for her central role as the source and nurturer of all life.

It did not take any great leap of the imagination for historians to suppose that on the morning of the winter solstice, some local sage or religious leader probably led the faithful from the farms around Newgrange into the central chamber of the mound. There, among the buried remains of their ancestors, they observed the great moment of renewal. With offerings and recitations, the community celebrated the astonishing gift of rebirth as the sun once again began its slow passage toward summer and held forth the promise of a new growing season.

How terribly important that moment must have seemed to warrant such an enormous construction project. The basic design of Newgrange is not particularly complicated, but its execution had to require an extraordinary effort. Simply moving the necessary

earth and stone to produce such a vast mound must have involved many months, perhaps years, of work by a virtual army of laborers. And, in the preliterate era in which Newgrange was constructed—a time characterized chiefly by the advent of agriculture, and otherwise by rather modest achievements—it was a prodigious accomplishment to have predicted exact celestial alignments, as the mound builders succeeded in doing. Perhaps equally impressive was their success in engineering a lasting network of underground passageways and chambers. Newgrange was clearly the work of people who cared deeply about the temple they were building. What is also clear is that the ancient farmers of Ireland held in awe the cosmic energies they honored with this monument and that they identified closely with those powers.

Although the Newgrange design is rather simple, it exemplifies one of the central obsessions of the prehistoric megalith builders in Europe. The people who erected the great stone circles and turned massive boulders on end to create natural spires were preoccupied with the need to ensure the continued fecundity of the earth. They believed that the energies contained in nature were of a sacred origin and that those energies derived from a literal coming together of heaven and earth. One of the most common symbols of this union revealed in the world's myths of creation is the shaft of the male principle penetrating and fixing in place the mound of the female principle. Precisely such an image was given form at Newgrange, where the mound is penetrated by a stone

passageway and the earth is recharged every year with light and power emanating from the heavens.

Judging by the archaeological evidence of civilizations before and after the Neolithic era, the sense of identification with the well-being of the earth exemplified at Newgrange was never limited strictly to concern about the planet's relationship with the sun. For people living close to the land, there was just as sure a sense that animals, plants, and especially trees interacted with one another and with human-kind in a mutually transactional world. These other forms of life were lesser beings, but they were far more than mere biological machines. It was believed, in fact, that all living things possessed a sort of conscious spirit. In many cultures, this deep-rooted sense of being partners on the earth with things not human was extended as well to geological features, such as stones, mountains, caverns, and brooks. These things are now regarded as purely inanimate objects, but in centuries past they were often thought of as some-how being conscious entities. They were spirits to be conversed with, cajoled, prayed to, and offered thanks. They came from the earth, as did the more obviously living crea-tures, and were thus linked to humanity by a commonly shared life force.

Such an outlook is hopelessly foreign to the majority of people today, especially to urban dwellers who normally have very little direct interaction with the natural world. But the ancient sensibility of living *with* the earth, rather than merely *on* it, has never disappeared altogether. To this day, for example, the Navajo Indians of the American Southwest consider themselves to be neither more nor less important than a sagebrush or a puff of wind. The various plants, animals, and things of nature are esteemed in traditional Navajo belief as "holy people," and the earth itself is regarded as a living, nurtur-ing, long-suffering mother.

The view of the earth as a living entity with an un-changing spirit or energy has circulated far and wide. The special areas where this spirit emerged or was felt most strongly were thought of as sacred places. And the ways in which people attempted to explore and live with the forces of the earth's spirit came to be expressed as principles of geomancy. People have long established guidelines for or-ganizing human settlements so as not to interfere with the forces inherent in the earth. One of the oldest and most in-stitutionalized of these geomantic systems is the Chinese tradition of *feng shui*. A more recent and up-to-date scien-tific discipline that addresses many of the same concerns is the branch of study called ecology.

As a growing number of scientists have concluded that the earth is seriously threatened as a habitat for human life, the viewpoints and forgotten knowledge of earlier times have seemed newly important and compelling. This is not to suggest that many biologists or meteorologists have thrown off their scientific ways to commune with the spirits of trees and mountains—although a few environmental ac-tivists and some devotees of the so-called New Age philos-ophies have done precisely that. But many in the scientific community have become so alarmed by what they take to be warning signs of global catastrophe—in particular, the thinning of the ozone layer in the earth's atmosphere and the gradual increase of temperatures around the globe—that they have gravitated to an oddly antiquarian outlook on the planet. Their new hypothesis, called Gaia, after an an-cient Greek deity who embodied the tradition of the Mother Goddess, holds that the entire planet is a living organism. Proponents of the new theory hope that by conceptualizing the earth in this manner they may find a way off the path to environmental calamity.

If the Gaia theorists are correct and the preservation of hu-man life is to depend on a return to an earlier world-view, there is at least hope in the fact that the traditional outlook has already proved wonderfully durable. In the fifteenth century, alchemist Basilius Valentinus gave expression to ideas that might just as easily have been the musings of philosophers in ancient Egypt or Neolithic Europe. "The earth is not a dead body," Valentinus wrote, "but is inhab-ited by a spirit that is its life and soul. All created things,

Science Takes Aim at an Old and Puzzling Phenomenon

Observed in fields worldwide, most often in rural Britain *(pages 6-15)*, crop circles like the one below still await a definitive explanation. In 1678, the broadsheet at right suggested the circles were the work of the devil. More recently, other speculators have blamed outer-space visitors—a theory that has drawn little support even from UFO research organizations.

Theories linking the mysterious swirls to field animals, birds, or unknown plant viruses have fared no better, because such organic causes fail to explain the sharply defined edges of the crop forms. And human hoax—though probably responsible in a few cases—is an unlikely explanation for the hundreds of crop circles reported before the rise of popular interest in the phenomenon.

To date, perhaps the most plausible explanation is one developed by British meteorologist Terence Meaden. According to his "plasma vortex" theory, rotating masses of positively charged air, created by winds flowing over hills, can twist crops into any of the reported circle patterns *(right)*. Meaden's theory might also account for the glowing lights and tingling sensations reported by some observers near recently formed circles.

Even the plasma vortex theory, however, fails to explain all. Yet to be addressed is the vexing question of how a vortex—acting in a few brief seconds—could bend but not break plant stems that snap like carrots in human hands.

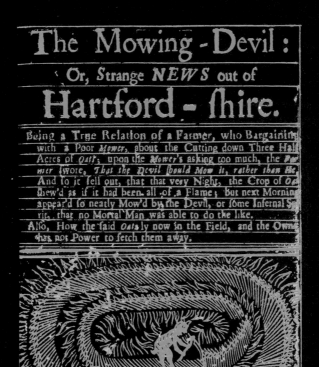

The Mowing - Devil :

Or, Strange NEWS out of

Hartford - fhire.

Being a True Relation of a Farmer, who Bargaining with a Poor Mower, about the Cutting down Three Half Acres of Oats; upon the Mower's asking too much, the Farmer fwore, That the Devil fhould Mow it, rather than He. And fo it fell out, that that very Night, the Crop of Oat fhew'd as if it had been all of a Flame; but next Morning appear'd fo neatly Mow'd by the Devil, or fome Infernal Spirit, that no Mortal Man was able to do the like.
Alfo, How the faid Oats ly now in the Field, and the Owner has not Power to fetch them away.

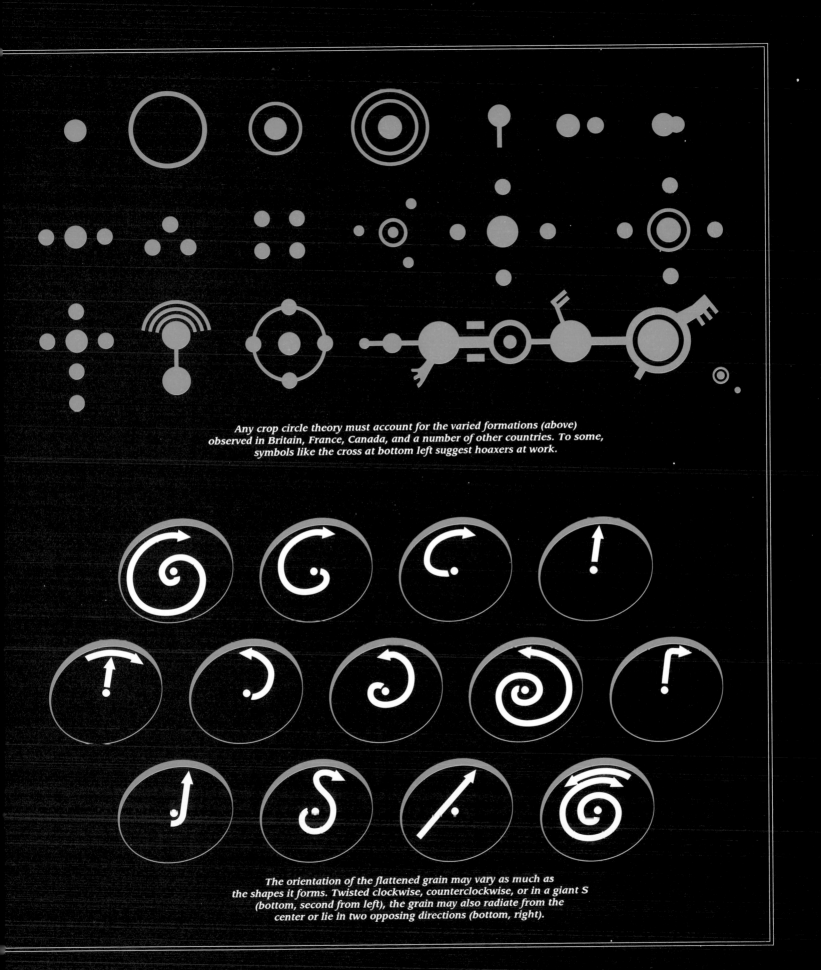

Any crop circle theory must account for the varied formations (above)
observed in Britain, France, Canada, and a number of other countries. To some,
symbols like the cross at bottom left suggest hoaxers at work.

The orientation of the flattened grain may vary as much as
the shapes it forms. Twisted clockwise, counterclockwise, or in a giant S
(bottom, second from left), the grain may also radiate from the
center or lie in two opposing directions (bottom, right).

minerals included, draw their strength from the earth spirit. This spirit is life, it is nourished by the stars, and it gives nourishment to all the living things it shelters in its womb." The alchemist's words reflect a message handed down to him in the myths that helped his forebears come to terms with their existence on earth. The crowning irony for these ancient races was that they lived on a planet that bestowed all life but that also insisted on taking it away.

In many of the oldest myths of creation, a female deity brings life to the earth directly out of her own body, and ever thereafter she is accountable for both the pain and the good in living. From Scandinavia to China, Africa, and the Americas, myths of such a goddess abound. One of the best known of the deities is the Greek Gaia, the goddess of the earth adopted by the ecology movement. Environmental activists pay her homage today when they display bumper stickers on their cars with a photo of the earth and the admonition "Honor Thy Mother."

In Greek mythology, Chaos was first to come into being, and next came the wide-bosomed Gaia. From Chaos emerged many troublesome things, including night, death, and uncertainty. But Gaia, the earth, bore out of her body the starry heavens, called Uranus. These became her equal and were great enough to cover her on every side. Then Gaia gave birth to the mountains, the hills, and the sea.

Chaos and its offspring continued to haunt the world, but Gaia made things tolerable by bringing about a countervailing order that imposed a certain logic within her domain. And then, from her union with Uranus, she brought forth her children the Titans, and thus began the familiar stories of Zeus and the many other deities who would direct the affairs of mortals. Though potent, and even present in that she was said to address humans through oracles, Gaia faded into the background as a relatively passive figure. She

had performed her work and retired from the field.

Hesiod, the earliest known chronicler of these deeds, harbored some rather unkindly thoughts about Gaia. It seemed to him that both the goddess and the world she represented were not always kind and bountiful. A Homeric hymn was more positive, however, because it told of the earth, the mother of us all "who feeds all that in the world exists . . . by thee, O Queen, are men blessed in their children, blessed in their crops." The poet went on to ponder a feature of the earth that has never failed to be noted in mythology: "Thine it is to give life and to take it back from mortal men."

If the Greek view of the goddess was marked by ambivalence, the reason may have been that the earth mother myth was inherited by storytellers such as Hesiod and Homer rather than invented by them. By the time the goddess reached Greece, her image had been drastically transformed—changes that had come about through a process familiar to scholars of mythology. It seems that succeeding generations and conquering dynasties routinely attempt to supplant the ideas of their predecessors or squelch the beliefs of their newly acquired subjects by killing off or denigrating the earlier deities. By the day of Hesiod and Homer, Greek theology was dominated by warlike male gods, and the goddesses had been shunted off into lesser roles.

As made clear by the ruins of Newgrange, however, and by a host of other archaeological discoveries, the role of the goddess was once anything but subservient. In Neolithic times, most societies envisioned the earth as female. The connection between the earth and a human mother's womb as places for the gestation of seeds was apparently too obvious to ignore. In fact, it seems that this feminine principle was well established much earlier, during the Paleolithic era. The world's museums are replete with tiny fig-

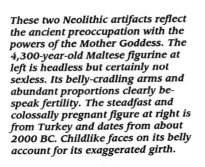

These two Neolithic artifacts reflect the ancient preoccupation with the powers of the Mother Goddess. The 4,300-year-old Maltese figurine at left is headless but certainly not sexless. Its belly-cradling arms and abundant proportions clearly bespeak fertility. The steadfast and colossally pregnant figure at right is from Turkey and dates from about 2000 BC. Childlike faces on its belly account for its exaggerated girth.

urines from that long-ago time that seem to demonstrate the importance of the goddess. The most famous of these relics is the Venus of Willendorf.

A 4⅜-inch statuette carved out of stone, the Venus has accentuated breasts and hips that leave no doubt she was a symbol of fertility. Scholars argue over the likelihood that she was also the image of a deity, but many are convinced she was, and a slightly later class of figurines leaves little room for skepticism. These carvings are realistic depictions of pregnant women, and some of them are wearing masks. In the artwork of this period, masks generally signified that the wearers were impersonating or shamanistically "becoming" deities, if only for the sake of ritual. Evidence suggests that by 7000 BC at the very latest, the worship of the earth as a goddess had become nearly universal. And for a period of perhaps five millennia, the analogy between the earth and the female body as the source of birth, nourishment, power, and protection dominated religious and artistic thought.

The potency of the concept of earth as mother is still evident in the goddess myths that have survived into our own times. No one ever put into words their feelings of attachment to the land more passionately than the Sioux Indian holy man Smohalla at the close of the nineteenth century. Railing against the ways of the Europeans who had settled in his native country, Smohalla asserted that it was "a sin to wound or cut, to tear or scratch our common mother by working at agriculture. . . . You ask me to dig in the earth? Am I to take a knife and plunge it into the breast of my mother? But then, when I die, she will not gather me again into her bosom. You tell me to dig up and take away the stones. Must I mutilate her flesh so as to get at her bones? Then I can never again enter into her body and be born again. You ask me to cut the grass and the corn and sell them, to get rich like the white men. But how dare I crop the hair of my mother?"

To Smohalla, the bones of his mother were the rocks of the earth, her flesh the soil, and her hair the vegetation. Parallels to the ideas he was expressing are found in other cultures. To this day, for example, many Polish peasants believe it a sin to turn over the soil before the end of March. Up until that time, it seems, the earth is considered pregnant. In many rural areas of Europe well into this century, it was thought that the souls of children yet to be born dwelled in the ground along with or as part of the earth's own spirit. And in the creation myths of many Native American tribes—the Navajo and the Zuni, to name just two—humanity spent a considerable part of its past in an unevolved, embryonic state. The bodies and souls of all humanity were said to be underground, in the womb of mother earth, whence they emerged to become part of the world we know.

The great Rumanian scholar Mircea Eliade, who wrote extensively on the history of religion and mythology, observed that stories of human beings who emerged directly from the earth have had almost universal distribution. In some languages, he noted, the word for "man" actually means "earth-born." Moreover, a great deal of folklore regarding babies who arrived from rivers, grottoes, swamps, and caves, delivered to their mothers by storks, frogs, fish, and other animals, has survived in twentieth-century superstitions. Related to these legends are beliefs involving special rocks or springs that have the power to help women who are seeking to conceive children. Eliade insisted that it was a mistake to dismiss such ideas as simple fairy tales or naive explanations for human procreation. "The reality is not so simple," he wrote. "Even among Europeans of today there lingers an obscure feeling of mystical unity with the native earth; and this is not just a secular sentiment of love for one's country or for the ancestors buried for generations around the village churches."

Eliade believed that embedded in the psyches of all men and women was a profound conviction that human life ultimately springs from the soil—in the same way that trees, flowers, or streams arise from the earth. This deep-seated instinctual knowledge, which he described as a "cosmobiological experience," gave people an overriding sense

The Enduring Mystique of the Pyramids

Thousands of years after their construction in the Egyptian desert, the pyramids continue to inspire legends of mysterious energies trapped in stone. Although none of the wonders attributed to them has been substantiated, the pyramids have shown that—at the very least—they have extraordinary powers in firing the imagination.

Long an important symbol for members of the Society of Freemasons, a pyramid was incorporated into the Great Seal of the United States by eighteenth-century Masonic patriots. The image still appears on the back of the one-dollar bill. In the 1800s, British Egyptologists discovered references to an ancient unit of length they called the pyramid inch. Calculations based on this abandoned system of measurement led to predictions of the world's end in 1874—an estimate later revised to 1914, 1920, and 1925.

By the time 1925 had come and gone, students of the paranormal had become intrigued by the pyramid shape. In the 1940s, French occultist Antoine Bovis visited Egypt and became convinced that stray cats that died inside the Great Pyramid underwent a process of mummification. He later claimed to have used a small wooden pyramid to preserve snakes, frogs, and lizards. Inspired by Bovis's experiments, Czech radio engineer

Karl Drbal invented a cardboard pyramid for storing razor blades. According to Drbal, blades stored in his container would stay sharp indefinitely.

Equally beneficial effects were reported by American movie star Gloria Swanson. In 1973, she told *Time* magazine that she slept with a miniature pyramid under her bed. Swanson claimed that the pyramid had such an effect that she generally awoke tingling "with every cell in my body." Researchers in California made similar assertions following tests in which subjects meditated in hollow pyramids. The E.S.P. Laboratory, a private Los Angeles firm, theorized that the structures served as "geometrical amplifiers," augmenting the powers of prayer.

Objective tests of pyramid power have not always borne out the enthusiastic claims. In Lille, France, a 1986 experiment tested the ability of pyramids to improve the quality of wine: A quantity of wine was divided in half and one group of bottles was kept for several days in a Plexiglas pyramid. The wines were then judged by a panel of experts who rated them on a scale of 1 to 4, and the pyramid-enhanced vintages edged out the ordinary ones by a score of 2.43 to 2.24. But this success was mitigated in a second trial, when the wines from the pyramid lost by a margin of 2.49 to 2.56.

of being rooted to the place of their birth. In Eliade's opinion, the claims of this intimate sense of belonging were far stronger than any possible demands of nationality or even family. Among other things, it made people long to be buried in their homeland.

Another great student of myth, the popular American scholar and commentator Joseph Campbell, believed that one of the very earliest abstract ideas entertained by prehistoric men and women was the concept of burial as a return to the womb for rebirth. Campbell cited as evidence certain findings in the graves of *Homo sapiens neanderthalensis,* a distant ancestor to our own species, whose time on earth lasted from perhaps 200,000 to 75,000 BC. Neanderthal graves were frequently provisioned with supplies for an afterlife, and the tombs were usually carefully oriented on an east-west axis, presumably because the sun was reborn on that path every day. Perhaps what is most telling, however, is the fact that the skeletons were frequently discovered bound in the fetal position. If Joseph Campbell's suppositions are correct, then it seems entirely likely that humanity's intimate sense of identification with the powers of the earth may have been inherited by the earliest representatives of our own species, *Homo sapiens.*

A great many customs and folk beliefs stemmed from this primal sense of connection and from the related concept of human mothers serving as surrogates for the mother earth. Among some tribes in the outlying regions of Australia, Africa, China, and South America, it is still considered advisable for mothers to give birth directly on the ground. A variation on this theme is for the mother to place her newborn on the earth immediately following its birth, so as to recognize the baby's true parentage. Among the Hopi Indians today, a child is not named until twenty days after its birth. As part of the naming ceremony, the infant is given a perfect ear of corn, referred to as its "mother corn." To the Hopi, this ear of corn is not merely a symbol of the Great Mother; it is an integral part of her and it is valued by the recipient throughout life as a spiritual guide. The naming ceremony is then completed by taking the infant outside at dawn to meet its spiritual father, the sun.

Mothers, of course, will occasionally grow angry at the misbehavior of their children, and the Great Mother was never considered an exception. Many different cultures have thought it necessary to offer sacrifices to the goddess of the earth in hopes of assuring the continued fecundity of the land or of smoothing things over before or after a terrible event, such as an earthquake or a drought. The Romans made a practice of sacrificing pregnant sows to Tellus, or Terra Mater. And in a few cultures, the observances were taken to an extreme and the sacrificial offerings were human. This was apparently the case among the Aztecs of Central America and in parts of ancient India.

In some cultures, the good mother earth was believed to represent justice or social conscience. There was one long-standing tradition among Slavic peasants, for instance, to call upon the earth as a witness in all legal disputes relating to land or property. If a litigant solemnized an oath by stating his point of view with a dirt clod on top of his head, the allegations were deemed incontestable. Similarly, certain African tribes relied upon the earth to avenge all breaches of morality. They believed, for example, that the very spirit of the earth was deeply offended by the spilling of human blood and would demand a sacrifice on the part of the offender as a means of atonement. A village official who was specifically devoted to such matters would assess the penalty, which might involve the killing of a goat or some other domestic animal. Interestingly, the wounded person or the family of a murder victim got nothing in such adjudications. The sole concern was to pacify the angry mother earth.

If the entire planet has been held sacred by some cultures, there have also been special places in every part of the world that were singled out because they seemed to help people feel that they were in tune with the energy or spirit of the earth. Like Newgrange, these locations were thought of as places where the powers of heaven and earth intermingled, and for that reason, they were held to be sacred. Quite often, these sites took on additional significance as they came to be known as places where godly wisdom was transmitted to humankind. It was through the coming together of the divine and the mortal, or so the story went, that people learned to feed themselves and ensure their access to all the necessities of life. The rituals celebrated on many holy grounds re-created the process by which such knowledge was acquired.

Sacred places run the gamut from locations of extraordinary natural splendor to rather ordinary sites such as rock ledges and groves of trees. Mountains have attracted their share of attention, which is understandable, perhaps, since they give the appearance of connecting the land and the sky. Many peaks have been revered as places where the heavens recharge the earth. For Christians, Golgotha, or Calvary—the place outside Jerusalem where Jesus was crucified—was the topmost point of a cosmic mountain and the site of Adam's birth and burial. It presented a neat conjunction of major biblical events, because the cross of Jesus Christ could be planted on top of the very grave of the man he was born to redeem. And the peak that Westerners call Mount Everest and view as a physical challenge to be conquered is known as Chomo-Lungma to the native people of Nepal, who cherish it as the mother mountain of the universe.

A common trait among many sacred places is that they are set off by clearly marked boundaries that distinguish the holy ground from the profane. In the view of Mircea Eliade, this emphasis on putting bounds between the two spheres was essential to the mystique of a sacred ground. It allowed believers to presume that the coming together of the divine and the mortal, which had consecrated the site in the first place, was not a one-time event but was instead an ongoing circumstance that continually filled the place with special power. Certain Indian tribes of North and South America have had a longstanding custom of returning to the sites that were deemed by tradition to be their ancestors' places of origin. They would make this journey in hopes of restoring their vitality by tapping the primal source of existence. As Eliade interpreted the practice, the holy place of the Indians became "an inexhaustible source of power and sacredness and enabled man, simply by entering

Two bronze Etruscan statuettes from the fourth and fifth centuries BC depict a priest and a plowman, both of whom had roles to play in the planning for a new city. The priest was instrumental in determining a propitious site and conducting rituals to placate the spirits of the earth. The plowman contributed by digging a trench where the walls of the city would be built. Offerings were then placed in the furrow to bring the city into harmony with the earth.

27

it, to have a share in the power, to hold communion with the sacredness."

In most religious traditions and folklore, hallowed places are not chosen by human beings but are somehow revealed to them. Sometimes the holy ground is discovered through the intercession of a saint or a hermit. El Hamma, for example, is a sacred site for some sects, located in the desert of central Tunisia. It is said to have made itself known when a sixteenth-century Muslim ascetic stopped there to rest for the night. Before going to sleep, the hermit thrust the end of his walking stick into the soft ground adjacent to a spring. When he awoke the next morning, he discovered that the stick had taken root and sprouted buds. The holy man took this as a sign that he should remain in the place to pursue his spiritual fulfillment. Comparable tales have cropped up in Christian lore and have given rise to some of that faith's most cherished shrines.

The discovery of other sacred places has depended on a bit more active searching and has sometimes revolved around portents that have been discovered in animal behavior. Apparently, some holy sites were determined by signs as seemingly trivial as the absence of insects or vermin. In other cases, an animal such as a bull was set loose to wander where it might for several days. When the beast was eventually hunted down, it was sacrificed immediately and the scene of the offering was thereafter considered to be special or hallowed ground. The most famous holy place ever revealed by an animal was the great Hellenic shrine at Delphi.

According to the chronicler Diodorus Siculus, goats were the first to discover the powers in the chasm that came to be the seat of the famous Delphic oracle. When the flocks would approach the edge of the ravine, they would bleat and leap about wildly. The curious shepherds went over to investigate, and they, too, reportedly experienced strange reactions, acting "for all the world like people possessed" and attempting to "prophesy the future." Although Delphi would become renowned as a wellspring of predictive powers, it seems that the overall effect of the place was not a gentle, meditative state of mind but what the Roman orator Cicero described as a "furor."

With people going mad and threatening to hurl themselves into the chasm, it soon became obvious that Delphi was a potentially dangerous place. Priestesses were appointed in hopes of harnessing the powers that seemed to be haunting the site. And so for many decades, a lone prophetess took her position by a specially designed bronze tripod, which the sages had devised to protect her during spells of divine possession. The Greeks believed that the prophecies that emerged from Delphi were transmitted in the form of a vapor, or pneuma, wafting up out of the chasm. They were also convinced—in the early days at least—that the ultimate source of both the pneuma and the revealed knowledge was none other than the Mother Goddess. Even in the later years of the oracle, when the special powers of the place were reevaluated and attributed to the male god Apollo, there remained a sacred precinct near the main temple that was given over to veneration of the earth goddess.

In Christian times, the oracle at Delphi fell into disuse, and numerous attempts have been made in the intervening years to explain its influence. Many people have at least partially accepted the original explanation of the Greeks, which attributed the oracle's power to natural exhalations of fumes from the earth set free by heavy rains or minor earthquakes. The great Scottish anthropologist and mythologist Sir James Frazer would only go so far as to say that the "frowning cliffs above Delphi and the deep glen below might naturally mark out the spot as a fit seat for a sanctuary and oracle of earth." In an effort to explain the decline of the oracle at Delphi, Plutarch compared its attenuating fortunes to the exhaustion of a silver or copper mine. Cicero, on the other hand, would have none of that: "You might think that they were talking of wine or pickles, which go off with time; but what length of time can wear out a power divine?"

Once revealed, by whatever means, sacred places

were generally distinguished from their surroundings by some sort of enclosure. Delphi was given its temple; Newgrange was protected by its mound; Stonehenge and many other sites were set apart figuratively by their great circles of stones. In addition to symbolizing the continuing presence of a divine force, such enclosures seem to have served as a warning that it was necessary to observe certain ritual preparations before approaching the holy ground. There was always a peculiar sense of danger associated with exposing oneself to a sacred site. In this regard, Mircea Eliade recalled the Lord's words to Moses: "Come not nigh higher, put off the shoes from thy feet: for the place whereon thou standest is holy ground." Removing shoes or washing feet outside a temple are two examples of modern carry-overs of the ritual "gestures of approach," as Eliade called them.

The swirls on this old English omphalos stone symbolize the earth's serpentine energies.

The sense of the power or danger inherent to a sacred place may have been related to the ancient practice of building walls around cities. At some point in history, the construction of human settlements began to take on many of the same ceremonial trappings that had sprung up around the holy monuments. In Eliade's view, every new human establishment was treated as a sort of mystical re-creation of the world. "If it is to last," he wrote, "if it is to be real, the new dwelling or town must be projected by means of the construction ritual into the 'center of the universe.' " One way of doing this, historians believe, was by building a wall around the center of the sacred site, and it is entirely possible that in ancient times the presumed magical utility of walls was considered every bit as important as their value as defensive fortifications. Walls divided the areas in which human organization had been imposed on the land and some semblance of the cosmic order established from the areas in which chaos still reigned.

In times of trouble, during outbreaks of disease or threats of invasion, people enacted a ritual in which they walked the perimeters of their walls and thus reinvoked the protective powers of the barriers. Such procedures were commonplace during the Middle Ages in Europe and India as well. A similar tradition is carried out to this day in parts of England and elsewhere in Europe. In a ceremony called the "beating of bounds," parishioners accompany their local clergy in a procession around the parish boundaries. By doing so, they reassert the belief that God has somehow specially blessed their land and can be counted on to protect its inhabitants. But the tradition is clearly a holdover from the ceremony carried out by their forebears to ritually lay claim to the powers of the earth.

Walls were only one of many ways in which the peoples of early civilizations tried to impose their control over the forces of nature. Throughout the ancient world, whenever sages endeavored to redirect the influences of a prominent sacred boulder or high priests performed a ritual at the center of a shrine, they were seeking more or less the same effect. They were trying to sustain the cosmic order by bargaining with the spirits of the earth and the sky. One scholar defined such mediation, or geomancy, as the attempt to put "human habitats and activities into harmony with the visible and invisible world." At one time, belief in the necessity of such measures was nearly universal, and vestiges of practices that arose in those times survive to this day, mostly in the form of religious ritual and folklore.

According to the old view, any change that was imposed upon the natural landscape could be expected to have serious repercussions. Even small transgressions, such as carelessly situating a building or a well, could lead to unforeseen and—quite possibly—unpleasant conse-

"Oyez, oyez, the glove is up," proclaims the town crier, opening
an English country fair in medieval fashion. He carries a glove-topped omphalos
pole, symbolic of a sanctuary for peaceful trade.

quences. A much-needed water supply might suddenly go dry, or a pasture might mysteriously go barren over the course of a winter. For the farmers of the British Isles, it was common practice down through the Middle Ages to plow deep furrows marking the boundaries of the fields that were under cultivation. The custom seems to have sprung from the same impulse that induced people to place enclosures around their sacred places. The furrow not only expressed ownership but magically "fixed" the spirit of the place and thereby ensured its fertility.

In recent times, archaeologists have noted that there are occasional breaks in these ancient ditches where the farmers appear to have lifted their plows for no readily apparent reason. Some scholars have suggested that the gaps may have been intended to serve as passageways for the spirit of the earth, allowing it to move unimpeded across the landscape.

Another trace of the influence of primitive geomancy can be seen in the care that ancient builders took to orient their shrines and domiciles relative to the points of the compass. The four cardinal directions—north, south, east, and west—were long believed to hold significant cosmological implications and were associated with the corresponding quadrants of the night sky (and thus were linked to astrological portents as well). In many societies, there were mythological guardians assigned to each quadrant of the heavens, and it became the task of these caretakers to protect the earth. In the Hebrew tradition, for example, the angels Michael, Raphael, Gabriel, and Phanuel were assigned the responsibility of upholding the throne of God and, with him, the central pillar of the universe. In Icelandic lore, the entire island was divided into four sections. Each quadrant was made up of three subdivisions, and the seat of government, which was known as the Althing, was situated at a fabled geomantic center of the land.

An archaic ritual is carried on in Saint Michael's parish of Oxford, England, as robed university faculty and students begin a ceremonial perambulation called the beating of bounds. Originally, the rite was performed to preserve a community's mystical lines of defense against invaders, either physical or spiritual.

It was always from the center that practitioners of geomancy planned the shapes of their buildings and towns. Many old churches in rural England were constructed on the remains of pagan temples. And in some cases, the Christian architects preserved the floor plans of the earlier structures. These clearly reflect the old beliefs in the importance of having a center and of carefully orienting the structure relative to that center. The basic plan in many old churches is a circle or a square set out around a central point marked by a stone called the omphalos. This term was taken from the Greek word for "navel" and carries connotations of birth and beginnings.

The idea of an omphalos predated by many centuries the building of medieval churches in England, and it has conveyed several different meanings throughout history. The omphalos was, first of all, a permanent, immobile point on the earth's surface that would serve as a link between the human and the divine. As such, it was closely related to the idea of creation and was an attempt on the part of the human community to tie itself to the sources of life and energy. An omphalos also marked a building as a sanctuary—a place of peace and organization. It was usually a stone, but it could also be a pillar, a wooden pole, or even a tree. Whatever its form, the omphalos conveyed the stability of a culture and the order that humans had wrought out of chaos. It was more than a mere act of anger, therefore, when Charlemagne chopped down the Saxons' omphalos pole, which was known to that people as the Irminsul. The conqueror was delivering an unambiguous sign that the old order was gone forever.

For centuries, geomantic principles such as building around centers and aligning to the points of the compass were at the heart of all city planning as people came together in ever-larger settlements. The Egyptian hieroglyph signifying the Ideal City was a circle divided in four equal parts. The symbol came to represent the Egyptian belief that a city was a microcosm of the earth, which in turn was a microcosm of the entire universe. And just as the earth was marked by its diversity, the quarters of the Ideal City were different from one to the next. Ideas very similar to this Egyptian belief seem to have sprung up independently in many parts of the world. Four-part designs are the fundamental planning schemes for cities as diverse as Teotihuacán, Baghdad, Winchester, Washington, D.C., and Beijing. In the Chinese capital, the emperor was ensconced at the center in the Forbidden City, site of the omphalos. Beyond the royal enclave was the secular city, which in turn was surrounded by the civilized provinces and beyond that the areas as yet entirely untamed.

The peculiarly Chinese form of geomancy known as feng shui that helped give shape to Beijing has had a profound and durable impact on China. Feng shui embodies a complex mélange of religious, philosophical, and mystical traditions. It incorporates astrology, analogy, ancestor worship, esoteric symbols such as the White Tiger and the Green Dragon, and some highly practical procedures for town planning and community hygiene, as well as attention to the elusive "breath" of nature, which is also referred to as *ch'i,* or *qi.*

Over the centuries, feng shui enabled the people of China to ensure that their empire, which was and is one of the most highly populated landscapes in the world, has also always remained one of the most visually pleasing. There have been times when the observance of feng shui has represented an impediment to technological progress; it was particularly decried as backward thinking during the Communist nation's Cultural Revolution of the late 1960s. And it is certainly true that the concern of the Chinese people for preserving the natural shape of the land has sometimes dampened their readiness to accept innovations such as railroads and modern highways. But numerous people are convinced that—on the whole—feng shui has been an enormous boon to China.

In recent years, a retired Chinese-American medical doctor, whose westernized training had led him to eschew all that even vaguely smacked of superstition, undertook a serious study of the traditional art of Chinese geomancy. He wound up becoming a steadfast proponent of feng shui and established a clinic to advise his California neighbors on how to improve their luck by making minor adjustments to their physical surroundings. When asked about the source of the magic's efficacy, the doctor admitted that he did not have a clue. "It works," was all he could say. He was not alone in his interest in this traditional art. Feng shui is currently enjoying a substantial revival in the United States and Western Europe.

One self-professed beneficiary of the old magic is restaurateur Johnny Kao, who is the proprietor of several successful businesses in and around Washington, D.C. When Kao opened a new restaurant in February 1983, business was at first extremely slow to build—and this despite enthusiastic reviews from the few customers Kao managed to attract. In frustration, he arranged for a visit by Lin Yun, a Chinese language scholar from Hong Kong, who was a practitioner of feng shui. The professor immediately set about analyzing the restaurant's physical layout and issued specific recommendations for improving the building's feng shui. At Lin Yun's behest, Kao agreed to hire a construction crew to build a new doorway at the center of the building, and within weeks business began to improve. Mr. K's, as the place is called, has done a thriving trade ever since, and Johnny Kao now insists that a feng shui consultation be part of the planning process for all his business ventures.

Kao's experience is an example of the application of feng shui principles for the benefit of individuals. For the growing band of Western environmentalists, city planners, and architects who have taken up the study of Oriental geomancy, the attraction lies more in feng shui's long history as an official "science" in China. For several centuries, feng shui experts were consulted as a matter of public policy and their teachings were promoted by the emperor, who established a governmental agency in what was then Peking called the Board of Rites. The sole responsibility of this body was to ensure that the feng shui perspective was taken into account in all public-works projects.

The Chinese geomancy is not, for the most part, characterized by exotic prescripts or beliefs. It has more to do with the mundane decisions of day-to-day living—where to plant trees, how to design livable interiors for homes and offices *(see pages 113-117)*. According to Chinese tradition, the earth and sky were created by the great forces of the two breaths—by the yin and yang, the inhalation and the exhalation, the male and female principles—but the work of creation can be completed only by the hands of human beings. Daily activity on the part of ordinary men and women is required to bring nature to its perfection. This would seem to be a generally upbeat and hopeful philosophy, but feng shui devotees are also quick to point out that there are risks involved in ignoring the natural laws at the root of their discipline. In their view, the decisions that people make in building homes, laying out cities, and carving roads into the countryside have a direct effect on the fortunes of the local population.

Feng shui is believed to have emerged as a full-blown methodology perhaps as little as a thousand years ago, during the Sung dynasty. Its roots stretch back much further, however, to one of the most ancient of Chinese practices—ancestor worship. In China, it has long been held true that one of the most potent of the invisible forces giving shape to an individual's fortunes was the continuing influence of that person's ancestors. Centuries before the birth of Christ, the Chinese already attached great importance to finding proper sites for the burial of ancestors. Once such sites were located, there were detailed prescriptions to be observed in conducting the actual burials. It was the practice, for example, to lay the bodies of the deceased with their heads pointing to the north—a direction associated with the male principle.

Before long, such considerations became institutionalized and were exercised as a matter of custom in funerals. For example, during the Han dynasty, an era that was marked by scholarship and centralized control and that extended from 207 BC to AD 220, the principles of feng shui were systematically collected and codified, and the rules that guided funerary practices were extended to the dwellings of the living as well.

By the time of the Sung dynasty, which lasted from 960 to 1126, there were several discernible branches of feng shui, some of which emphasized subtle concerns about the twofold breath and searched for mythological shapes in the natural landscape. Others focused on the overall order of nature and sought meaning in the numerical proportions revealed in natural objects. By the nineteenth century, when a British missionary named Ernest Eitel wrote a book on feng shui that brought the Chinese geomancy to the attention of people in the Western world, the philosophy had become an intimate part of daily life in China. It affected everything from funerals and weddings to road construction and flower arranging.

The influence of feng shui had become so pervasive that the Chinese looked upon the whole of their country as one great sacred landscape. Within this idealistic vision, it became the goal that everything set in place by human hands should be fashioned in response to the forms and forces of nature. In the eyes of the geomancers, moreover, the natural landscapes took on a life of their own. The shapes of dragons and tigers discernible everywhere in the rise and fall of the land were more than mere symbols or ideas—they were living geological beings, exerting their influence over the land and emitting lines of force outward from their extremities. Where such lines crossed, the geomancers expected to find places of particular power and spiritual resonance.

The ultimate goal of feng shui is to produce the optimal flow of qi, the ever-present spirit of the earth. And therein lies the problem for most Westerners who have been exposed to the teachings of this system. There is a distinct difficulty in trying to integrate concepts such as the earthly qi and the cosmic breath with a scientific understanding of nature. From the mainstream Western perspective, all forces or energies should be explainable in terms of the laws of physics. But for admirers of feng shui, this is not a great concern. For

them, there are certain forces, such as the eroding power of wind and water, that do indeed lend themselves to description by scientists. Yet there are other influences, some just as potent in giving shape to the land, that are not so easily explained. And from the traditional feng shui perspective, every form of power or energy that affects the earth must be treated as a whole.

In many ways, the art of feng shui is analogous to the practice of acupuncture, a system that arose from the same basic tenets and values. In acupuncture, doctors or therapists actively interfere with the flow of various sorts of energy through the human body in an effort to bring them into harmony. Feng shui provides guidelines for achieving the same result, except that the harmony occurs within a building or over the body of the land.

Although the mystical currents of energy that are so integral to feng shui and acupuncture are mostly foreign to the Western perspective, they are not entirely unknown. In recent years, a comparable notion of telluric energy—a kind of natural electrical current that is coursing through the crust of the earth—has been attached to the theory of ley lines. These are hypothetical tracks or paths dating from very ancient times and connecting the sites once held sacred by cultures long since vanished. The idea of ley lines was first proposed in 1921 by a Welsh businessman named Alfred Watkins.

Watkins was an amateur student of history and an avid explorer of ancient sites. After spending a number of years traveling through the outlying regions of western England and Wales, he arrived at the conclusion that many of the pre-Roman landmarks discovered in the British Isles had been purposely aligned in rows that ran dead straight across the countryside. He applied the name "ley" to his finding, borrowing the old Saxon term for a meadow, or a cleared strip of land. Apparently, several other Europeans of the 1920s had arrived at similar conclusions on their own, and Alfred Watkins's theory—which was rejected out of hand by the majority of historians—was greeted with enthusiasm in some quarters.

For nearly two decades, the process of charting new ley lines was a passionate pursuit for scattered groups of freethinking historians and hobbyists. They corresponded, held meetings, and even formed an international alliance of sorts, called the Old Straight Track Club. Some of the lines they identified ran for many miles and passed through eight or more presumed holy places—through burial mounds, monoliths, sacred groves, and old churches built on the sites of earlier pagan temples.

Alfred Watkins's theory was that the ley lines simply marked the trading routes of early times, but not all ley enthusiasts were in agreement on this issue. It was pointed out that while some of the lines ran between more or less obvious destinations and could have been of use to wandering merchants or traders, many others crossed precipitous terrain where practical people would never have attempted to engineer paths or roads.

Nowadays, some who have studied the subject hold the view that Watkins's tracks actually trace the channels of earth's natural telluric energy. According to this theory, the people who constructed prehistoric monuments were much more closely attuned to the forces of nature than modern-day builders and could somehow sense the places where earth's energy was particularly strong. They may have situated their structures on such high-energy sites.

Such a hypothesis is of course very difficult to prove, but its supporters find its implications too important to ignore. It has led, among other things, to a renewed interest in the sacred places of the past. At the great shrines of the European megalith builders—at Newgrange, Stonehenge, Avebury, and many other sites—investigators ranging from dowsers and psychics to astronomers and historians search for signs of the elusive energy, trying to puzzle out the schemes of the ancients for harnessing the earth's forces. For many others, the search for contact with the spirit of the planet takes—literally—a more down-to-earth form, as they seek the magic power in the individual elements that make up the physical world.

Living in the Land of the Gods

Traditionally, the American Indian never even considers the notion "that he is independent of the earth, that he can be severed from it and remain whole," wrote N. Scott Momaday, himself a Kiowa. "The earth is sacred. . . . It is a living entity . . . he is bound to the earth forever in his spirit."

When Native Americans speak of the sacred earth, they mean more than just soil and rocks. Their concept of the hallowed land includes plants, animals, the sky with its sun and stars, as well as weather phenomena. In this world-view, humans must not disturb the balance of the elements or disorder will result.

And yet there is more to the Indian belief in the earth's power than even this age-old message. Native Americans have long held certain places to be especially holy, suffused with a mystical, spiritually tangible power. The Hopi Indians say these spots are energized by a spirit named Palongawhoya beating on a drum; the vibrations of his drumbeats surface most noticeably at the holy places. One area in Arizona's San Francisco Peaks, revered by both Hopi and Navajo, was revealed in a geological study to have a *physically* tangible special energy: an exceptionally strong telluric current, the electrical flow through the earth's surface generated by the planet's magnetic field. A possible explanation is that rocks in the area have unusually low electrical resistance.

Nowhere are Native American sacred places more spectacular than in the Southwest. There the lives and souls of the region's Indians have long been intricately connected to formidably beautiful landmarks like the ones on the following pages.

Wind-Carved Towers of the Navajo Spirits

Because its towering wind-carved buttes resemble man-made structures, European-Americans named this stark and beautiful place Monument Valley. The Navajo, who have known it longer and far more intimately, call it Land of Room Enough and Time Enough.

In their tradition, the vast expanse of flatlands and tall stone formations, which straddles the Utah-Arizona border, is not the unpopulated territory it appears. The Navajo say that each of the buttes is occupied by its own distinct spirit and that the whole valley is sacred ground. Navajo shamans still say prayers and leave offerings at the formations of particular spirits they wish to appease or whose assistance they seek.

The Flying Rock That Rescued an Indian Tribe

A dark volcano-spewed mass worn into its present shape by winds, New Mexico's Ship Rock was so named by European-Americans for its resemblance to a sailing vessel. But the Navajo call the 1,400-foot formation Tse bit'a'i—rock with wings.

They say their ancestors once sought refuge from attacking enemies atop the rock, which at that time was located some distance from its present position. When the Indians prayed for deliverance, declare the Navajo, the rock suddenly sprouted wings and flew across the sky, carrying the tribe to safety at the place where it now stands.

Sacred Lair of the Spider Woman

Soaring 800 feet above the floor of Arizona's Canyon de Chelly, Spider Rock—the formation at far right—is considered by the Hopi to be the home of Spider Woman. They say she helped create them and assisted their emergence into the fourth world, the last existence before an Armageddon-like purging that will lead to a new cycle of worlds.

The Navajo call the prominence at left in this picture Speaking Rock because of its mouthlike cleft. They sometimes threaten misbehaving children that Speaking Rock will tell their names to Spider Woman, who will snatch them away and leave them on top of Spider Rock forever.

The Waters of an Enchanted Canyon

Havasu Canyon, with its cascading falls and lush vegetation, provides a startling contrast to the rest of the arid Grand Canyon. The Havasupai Indians, who trace their ancestry to the clairvoyant shamans of the Colorado River Yuman, have inhabited this oasis for centuries, using the water to irrigate their little patches of vegetables and fruits. They consider the canyon, and especially the springs that feed the creek and falls, to be sacred, regularly making offerings of tobacco, peaches, or corn.

The Havasupai say that the canyon walls used to close in and crush anyone passing through. One story tells of two young boys who went into the canyon looking for reeds to make arrows. When the canyon began to close on them, they wedged two long juniper logs between the walls—which, the Havasupai claim, have been held open ever since.

Bringing Turquoise to the Taos Fount of Life

The frigid, turquoise water of Blue Lake, high in northern New Mexico's Sangre de Cristo Mountains, is believed by the Taos Indians to be the source of all life and the final resting place for their souls. In 1906, the lake and surrounding lands were taken from the tribe by the U.S. government and made part of Carson National Forest. In 1971, after decades of disruption and desecration, the sacred lake and 48,000 acres of wilderness were returned to Taos Pueblo ownership—and by some accounts just in time. An Indian legend says that if the Taos people should "someday be forced to leave their homes, or if they should by their own accord give up their pueblo and their land, then the world will end." Each year the Indians make pilgrimages to the lake, tossing in bits of precious turquoise as offerings to the sacred waters.

The Rainbow Bridge That Turned to Stone

Rainbow Bridge, at 309 feet the highest natural arch in the world, became the focus of a whole religion. The Navajo say the bridge was formed when a spirit heard the prayer of another supernatural being, who was trapped by a flood. He hurled down a rainbow, and as the threatened spirit raced across it to safety, it turned to stone beneath his feet. For centuries, adherents of the Rainbow religion trekked to the bridge to make offerings and pray. But when the Glen Canyon Dam made the once remote site easily accessible by boat, it became too crowded with tourists for the Navajo worshipers, and the practice faded away—although the faith may still exist.

A Window at the Center of the World

This stone formation with a hole in its center was called Tségháhodzání—perforated rock—by the Navajo. But its location near Winslow, Arizona, was known as Niʾʾalniiʾgi (earth's center). A spring beneath the rock was one of four sources of water used in the waterway ceremony, performed to secure abundant rain.

In 1936, the federal government chose this site for its Navajo Central Agency. The bureaucrats—noting that apart from constructing a radio station, administration building, employee residences, and a golf course, "nothing further was done to alter the native scenery"—continued to call the place Niʾʾalniiʾgi. When the Navajo objected, the community was rechristened Window Rock.

CHAPTER 2

Earth, Air, Fire, and Water

When psychiatrist Carl Jung was growing up in Switzerland, his most cherished friend was a rock. The seven-year-old Jung, who along with Sigmund Freud would eventually help establish the practice of psychoanalysis, discovered an agreeable spot on a particular boulder in the garden of his family home and whiled away the hours there, lost in childhood reveries. A lonely, introspective youngster, he developed such a strong affinity for this place—for "my stone," as he called it affectionately—that he would sometimes have a hard time remembering whether he was the person sitting on the boulder or he was the boulder himself and someone was sitting on him.

A few years later, while still in grade school, Jung carved the end of a wooden ruler into the shape of a human figure. He then found a smooth, oblong black stone that had washed up on a bank of the Rhine, and he painted it with secret symbols and bundled it, together with the little carved man, into an old pencil box. In boyish fashion, he hid the box in the attic—a place he was forbidden to go—and told no one of his secret. Occasionally, he would slip up to the attic to visit the toys, and he came to equate the painted stone with his well-loved boulder in the garden. Even when he could not be near his hidden treasures, he felt a deep and inexplicable satisfaction in simply remembering them. Their memory, it seems, helped him cope with the anxieties of a troubled childhood.

In his autobiography, published more than seventy years later, Jung recalled the solace he derived from the little wooden man and the magic stone. "In all difficult situations," he wrote, "whenever I had done something wrong or my feelings had been hurt . . . I thought of my carefully bedded-down and wrapped-up manikin and his smooth, prettily colored stone." Only much later, as an adult doing research on the power of symbols, did he learn that Australian Aborigines and other primitive peoples kept similar "soul stones," or churingas, as their secret talismans. With this in mind, Jung developed a theory that the figure he had carved as a boy had served him as a *kaabir,* which is a sort of personal deity. He also guessed that the stone he had taken from the river had infused his handmade, personal deity with a spark of the cosmic life force.

Jung's childhood fixation on his rock, his kaabir, and his painted stone would greatly influence his later theories. He came to believe that all human beings, living and dead, were connected by a collective unconscious—a world spirit, or *spiritus mundi*—that arose from the earth. Rocks, water, trees, and other physical components of the earth were, in his view, the points of contact that enabled humankind to communicate with the world spirit. For Jung, his own empathy for the things of nature reflected an instinctual sensitivity to the earth's life force. He believed that all people were capable of such feelings, and he considered them an important part of the human psychic makeup.

There is a great deal of historical evidence that sheds light on Jung's views in these matters. The earliest human societies worshiped earth deities—most often characterized as female—who regulated the visible and invisible workings of the land and the sky. Later religions worshiped different gods, but interest in the forces that had shaped the planet endured and prompted a succession of theories about the structure of earth and its parts. One of the most enduring explanations of this sort was put forth in the fourth century BC by the Greek philosopher Aristotle. All matter, he declared with finality, was composed of varying proportions of four basic elements: earth, air, fire, and water.

Today, scientists know that Aristotle's elements are themselves made up of infinitely smaller building blocks called atoms, which arrange themselves in complex structures. They also realize that each individual atom comprises a dizzying variety of sub-

atomic particles with odd names such as protons, leptons, and quarks. Yet Aristotle's theory of the four elements—which held sway for nearly 2,000 years—did not entirely miss the mark. If it is interpreted broadly enough, in fact, it still provides a sort of intuitively pleasing explanation for the workings of nature.

All of the elements known to modern science can, under suitable conditions of heat and pressure, assume forms corresponding to the Aristotelian elements. Iron, for example, usually exists as a solid—not unlike the soil of the earth. But it can also become a molten liquid like water or a gas like the air. Moreover, locked into every atom of iron is an enormous amount of nuclear energy, and that energy can be thought of as the rough equivalent of fire. In a sense, therefore, Aristotle's four basic elements sum up all the physical states that iron can assume, and they sum up as well the range of possibilities for all other materials in nature. More important, the special significance of earth, air, fire, and water was taken as gospel for many centuries by scientists, philosophers, and common people alike. And in the course of that time, each of the four Aristotelian elements came to be seen as a manifestation of the earth's energy or spirit.

None of the other three elements has been the object of quite so much reverence and superstition as has the earth. Primitive societies worshiped mother earth not only as a fecund provider and nurturer whose powers were observable in natural things but also as a living spirit inhabiting specific earthly locations. From the beginning, rocks of all kinds were looked upon as favored resting places for the spirit of the earth. Consequently, rocks large and small were invested with all sorts of magic powers by the people of many different races and cultures. Trees and plants, animals and other living things, even dirt and sand were part of the earth's inventory, but they were never considered to be of the earth so elementally as rock. Stone was everything human flesh was not: solid, unyielding, and—to all appearances—immutable and everlasting. It was utterly reliable, and it neither wept nor bled.

Some particular stones have exercised great power over the human imagination. For the millions of Muslims who make up approximately one-fifth of the world's population, there is no object on earth more sacred than a smallish black rock enshrined in a sanctuary called the Ka'ba at Mecca in Saudi Arabia. Eight inches in diameter, the sacred black stone is in fact a meteorite, the spent remains of an asteroid that flamed through the earth's atmosphere thousands of years ago. The Islamic religion teaches that the stone was given by Allah to Abraham, the patriarch of all Muslims. Islamic tradition also holds that the stone was part of the first house of worship dedicated to a single God. The treasure now rests, framed in silver, in the southeastern corner of the Ka'ba.

Five times each day, Muslims all over the globe turn toward Mecca and the Ka'ba to pray, but it is the dream of every devout follower of Muhammad to journey to Mecca on a pilgrimage, or hajj. The culmination of a hajj is to walk seven times around the Ka'ba, and the ambition of every one of the two million or so pilgrims who visit Mecca each year is to touch or kiss the black stone. According to the lore that surrounds the great relic, its surface has been worn smooth by the lips of the millions of believers who have kissed it, as Muhammad is said to have done some thirteen centuries ago.

The black stone has become the Islamic omphalos: In the eyes of Muslims, it marks not only the center of the world but also the gate of heaven. The historical impor-

tance of omphalos stones like the one in Mecca goes well beyond their function as religious or ceremonial landmarks. In a number of early societies, the first cities germinated from sanctuaries built at the site of an omphalos. As a particular cult or religion flourished, its central complex of temples expanded and attracted more and more secular enterprise. Gradually, urban complexes were established in locations that had begun as purely religious sites. In some cases, therefore, sacred stones served as the seeds of urban civilization.

The analogy between omphalos stones and seeds carries over to the fact that the center-marking stones were often placed beneath the earth in caves. Caverns, rock fissures, and grottoes have always been associated in mythology and folklore with the life force of the earth. While mountains, in their distant sunlit grandeur, were viewed as natural symbols of the earth's fertile energies, caves represented a darker side of those same forces centered in the underworld.

Even before people learned to give names to their gods and to establish patterns of worship, caves played an important role in human development. They were home to countless generations of early humanoids who learned to evict the fierce four-legged animals that were their rivals for shelter within the earth. But when *Homo sapiens* developed a spiritual awareness, caves were invested with a mystical importance that went far beyond their usefulness as ready-made shelter. Many religions, from ancient times to this day, have perpetuated the belief that the subterranean vaults were gateways to a lower kingdom in which the earth goddess made her home.

The Apache Indians of Arizona regard as sacred the Superstition Mountains, east of Phoenix, partly because of an old legend passed along by their forebears. The story suggests that somewhere in that hilly terrain is a cave leading down to the interior of the earth. The entrance to this cave is said to be guarded by a nine-headed snake that will let no human being pass. And the winds spewing up from the underworld through this hole are presumed to be the

Seeking to placate the spirits of Lake Barombi Mbo in Cameroon, members of a secret Bantu society prepare an offering of chicken blood. Many villagers attribute all water-related troubles—including the periodic spread of deadly lake-water gases—to the anger of Mammy Water, a spirit living in the lake.

cause of the severe dust storms that bedevil the Indian lands from time to time.

Early Greek and Roman settlements grew up around sites in which oracles allegedly passed along the wisdom of the gods. Many of the oracles, including the famous one at Delphi, were enshrined in or near caves, whose dark depths reinforced the impression of a holy and powerful place. One influential oracle was established at Trophonious, an old religious site near Mount Helicon in the Greek district of Boeotia. According to legend, anyone who made the dreadful descent to confront the earth goddess in her cave at Trophonious could never hope to smile again.

One of the most important religious centers for the Greeks was at Eleusis, not far from the great city of Athens. This ancient settlement was the site of the renowned Eleusinian mysteries, which were described by such luminous Greek and Roman writers as Homer, Plutarch, and Sophocles. The rites celebrated at Eleusis were performed in honor of Demeter, the goddess of agriculture and fruitfulness. At the heart of the Eleusinian sanctuary was a cave, called the Plutonion, and an omphalos stone that was said to bring together the energies of the underworld and the regions known to mortal men and women. Beginning in the sixth century BC, the Eleusinian mysteries flourished for nearly a thousand years. And the omphalos at Eleusis came to embody for the Greeks their most profound feeling for the earth as the source of all fertility and wonder.

In addition to marking the center of the universe and staking out the places where the divine and mortal realms coincide, stones have performed many other roles in helping human beings come to terms with their place in the world. The giant upright slabs of rock at Stonehenge and other megalithic sites in Britain and France were originally parts of enormous astronomical tools for predicting the spring and fall equinoxes. They helped ancient peoples mark the changes of the seasons and observe the moments when the sun changed course in its trek across the heavens.

The argument is sometimes put forward that the an-

cient builders who erected the great stone monoliths worked with rock because it was the only material they had available. Had steel, aluminum, or concrete been ready at hand—or so this line of reasoning goes—the monument builders would have probably chosen one of them instead. But it seems clear that the great slabs of rock used in Stonehenge, at least, were chosen for reasons that went far beyond mere convenience.

The underpinning of the great Salisbury Plain in which Stonehenge is situated is mostly chalk, a soft limestone composed of the remains of countless tiny seashells. The shells were deposited as sediment during the thousands of years in which the plain was part of the seabed. In some places, however, a layer of much harder rock formed over the chalk, and as this stratum of stone eroded, it split and cracked to form giant angular blocks with fairly straight edges and faces. The shapes of these slabs would have been impossible for the stoneworkers of old to achieve with their rudimentary bone and stone tools, and it is likely that they were filled with awe by the great blocks that nature had formed. If so, there was a certain logic to the assumption that the slabs were imbued with a special power, and the builders were right to put them to use in their temples. The immense circles of stones that the Druids erected, and that still stand mute on the Salisbury Plain, attest to the strength of this conviction.

Similar but smaller stone structures are scattered throughout many other parts of Britain and France. Brittany in northern France, where the Celtic people lived several millennia ago, is littered with almost 5,000 such megaliths. Some of them are solitary upright spires called menhirs— the name is a combination of the old Breton words *men* meaning "stone" and *hir* meaning "long." There is evidence that the menhirs were very carefully situated to achieve particular spiritual or mystical goals. Another type of megalith is the dolmen, which consists of two or more vertical stones crossed by a horizontal slab. *Dol* is the Breton word for "table." The dolmens apparently served as burial places and were intended not only to protect the

According to Polynesian tradition, the spiral tattoos on the face of this Maori
tribesman will ensure him safe passage to the world of the dead. After death, the islanders
believe, a fearsome hag eats the spirals and thereby frees the soul from the body.
If she finds no such tattoos, she will eat the eyeballs instead.

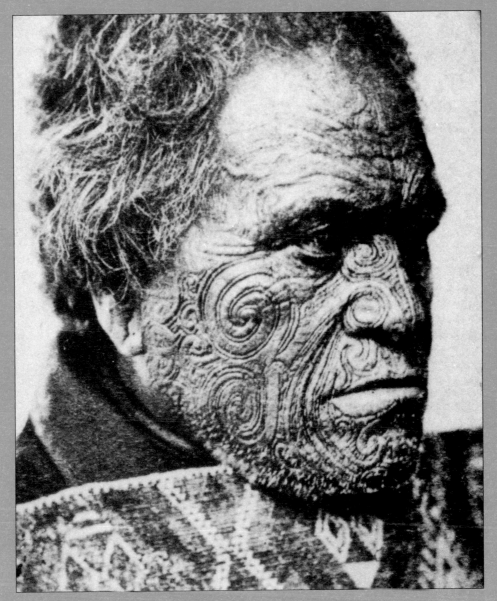

Framed by a rectangle of boulders on a field of white stones, this austere shrine in Takihara, Japan, is intended to bring Shinto worshipers closer to their dead and to the nature gods they call kami. In Shinto belief, the kami include all manner of natural things and phenomena, ranging from the sun and the moon to animals and plants, thunder, winds, earthquakes, and ordinary rocks.

physical remains but also to provide shelter for the souls of the departed.

Many secrets still haunt Brittany's ancient dolmens, which date back thousands of years before the Christian era began, but there is nothing dated about the practice of planting vertical stones for spiritual purposes. Less than a few hours' drive from the celebrated megalithic ruins at Carnac stretches the coast of Normandy. There, in gleaming rows, stand forests of stark crosses marking the tombs of thousands of soldiers who lost their lives during the Allied invasion of France in 1944. Like the enduring Celtic dolmens of Brittany, these modern tombstones were lovingly shaped from stone. They were intended to stand forever as guardians of the spirits of people whose bodies had been returned to earth.

Stones with alleged special powers have been put to more prosaic uses as well. Rocks with natural holes in them were believed to be magical in many different cultures. In Britain, such stones or pebbles were known variously as hag stones, witch stones, and mare stones. A holed rock suspended over a bed was believed to protect its owners from witchcraft and to ward off nightmares, rheumatism, and night sweats. If the stone was hung behind the front door, it was believed to keep evil spirits out of the house; tied to a door key, it worked together with the iron in the key to provide a powerful antidote to bad luck.

Even stronger magic was attributed to larger rocks and boulders marked by natural holes. In the French village of Fouvent-le-Haut, parents pass their newborn babies through the opening in such a stone, and they believe that the ritual ensures happiness for the children and guards against evil spells. Some of the early inhabitants of India looked upon stones with holes in them as symbols of the *yoni,* or womb, of the world. In their view, the act of passing the body through such a hole was like a prayer for regeneration according to a great feminine principle. In Cornwall, England, the so-called Crick or Creeping Stone was associated with more down-to-earth concerns. Sufferers with back pains believed that they could cure their lumbago if they crawled nine times through the hole in this stone, always with their faces to the sun.

Stones have also been associated with fertility in many regions of the world. Women in southern India, for example, believed that they could induce conception by rubbing against certain holy stones that they associated with their ancestors. Anthropologists have noted similar practices occurring among Australian Aborigines, California Indians, and the peoples of New Guinea and Madagascar. And as late as the 1880s—at the height of the supposedly prudish Victorian era—childless husbands and wives would strip to the buff and dash around a reputedly enchanted stone near Carnac in northwestern France. To ensure conception, this bizarre ritual was carried out in the company of the couple's relatives.

In addition to stones promoting good health and fertility, the pharmacopoeia of folk medicine has long found a place for such mundane curatives as clay, mud, and sand. Taken internally or used as a poultice, sometimes in combination with other ingredients such as lemon juice, vinegar, or mustard, clay has been prescribed for a wide range of physical complaints. It has factored in the treatment of dysentery, worms, ulcers, constipation, cholera, carbuncles, burns, and arthritis. In widely scattered areas of the world today, clay containing iron and other minerals essential to health is rolled into tiny balls, baked, and gulped down like vitamin pills.

The effectiveness of using clay as a medicine was widely proclaimed by early physicians, among them the famous eleventh-century Arab "prince of doctors," Avicenna, whose writings were circulated extensively in Europe. And clay continues to attract proponents among modern Western physicians. They believe that the substance somehow functions as a strong positive element in flushing from the body toxic elements that emit negative radiations. Although there is a paucity of clear scientific evidence in support of these claims, there seems to be little doubt that the mud does have certain therapeutic effects. Its modern champions assert that clay acts as a stimulant or catalyst in helping

the internal organs to mend themselves. Supporters of this view speak of clay as the "living earth" and believe that its power is derived from the living planet that is its source. Even in small amounts, they claim, clay retains the potent healing energy imparted to it by the magnetic force of the earth as a whole.

To the scientists of earlier times, one of the most perplexing enigmas regarding the planet that provides these natural curatives had to do with the shapes of the earth's continents. As long ago as 1620, when the art of cartography had become sufficiently advanced to produce reasonably accurate maps, the English philosopher Francis Bacon made a puzzling observation. He noticed that if the shape of South America was tilted slightly and placed against an outline of the African coast, the two continents fit together as neatly as the pieces of a jigsaw puzzle. Bacon, of course, had no way of explaining this curious fact.

The question hung unanswered for more than 300 years. In the nineteenth century, scientists discovered that the eastern and western hemispheres have similar rock formations and fossils. This was tantalizing evidence that the continents located in the two hemispheres may have once been continuous, but no reputable scientist was willing to go out on a limb to defend such a radical idea. Then in 1912 a German meteorologist named Alfred Wegener proposed that all the earth's landmasses were once joined in a vast supercontinent. Wegener called this enormous body of land Pangaea, a Greek word meaning "all earth," and he suggested that over a period of millions of years, the known continents had drifted apart. Most geologists dismissed out of hand Wegener's theory of "continental drift." In part, they demurred because Wegener was a meteorologist rather than one of their own. But they also could see no feasible mechanism to account for such a movement of landmasses.

Despite criticism and even ridicule, Wegener clung to his theory right up to the time of his death in 1930. And over the next thirty years, evidence would accumulate to vindicate his confidence in the theory. Among the discoveries made during that period was the astonishing realization that a mountain range 46,000 miles long runs like a giant scar along the bottom of the world's oceans. Geologists call this feature the mid-ocean ridge. Samples of the seafloor collected by research ships, meanwhile, showed that the ocean bottom is volcanic in origin and much younger than the continents.

In the 1960s, Princeton geologist Harry Hess and others pulled all the evidence together in a compelling theory that came to be known as plate tectonics. According to Hess's scenario, the earth's upper layer consists of some twenty "plates," or crustal sections. The continents, composed of slightly lighter materials than the rest of the earth's crust, "float" like corks embedded in the plates. The plates, in turn, are formed out of magma, or molten rock, that has hardened after oozing up from the underlying mantle of the earth at the mid-ocean ridge. Energized by currents of magma that continuously circulate through the mantle, the plates move ponderously away from the ridge, carrying the continents along with them.

When two plates collide, the edge of one section is driven beneath the edge of the other and into the mantle of the earth. The gargantuan force of such a collision may cause the continental crust to wrinkle in the form of a mountain range, and it usually results in an enormous buildup of pressure. The pressure can then only be equalized by a release of energy, and this brings about the violent phenomenon of earthquakes—perhaps the most extraordinary manifestation of the energy that resides in the earth. Anyone who has ever experienced a major earthquake can attest to the feeling of panic it is likely to inspire. Few things are taken more for granted than the solidity of the earth. Terra firma, the Romans called it. And when something so seemingly secure begins to behave in an unexpected way, the experience is profoundly unsettling.

Other phenomena associated with earthquakes sometimes contribute to the overriding sense of gloom or foreboding. Survivors occasionally report seeing an aurora-like glow in the sky, blue flames hovering over the land, or giant fireballs flying overhead. They tell of hearing disturbing sounds such as loud groans, explosions, rumbling, grating, whistling, or screeching. Some of these noises are probably caused by the rending of stone along the fracture line. But scientists have proposed a much stranger explanation for some of the sounds that accompany earthquakes. They believe that in a major tremor the ground may vibrate like the skin of a giant kettledrum. As it rises and falls ten feet or more, it may be generating seismic sound waves that reverberate in the atmosphere.

Some biblical scholars have proposed that an earthquake might actually have been responsible for the parting of the Red Sea that enabled Moses and the Israelites to escape their captivity in Egypt. In a similar vein, some people believe that the "fire and brimstone" credited in Scripture with destroying the corrupt cities of Sodom and Gomorrah may have been caused by large amounts of natural gas and sulfur released during an earthquake and ignited by hearth fires or lightning.

One of the persistent bits of folklore surrounding earthquakes is that animals can sense them before they occur. For thousands of years, observers have described the strange behavior of dogs, cats, horses, cattle, elephants, birds, frogs, fish, and even ants and bees in the minutes, hours, or days prior to an earthquake. In AD 373, the Roman naturalist Aelian described how mice and snakes had fled a city five days before an earthquake struck. And in 1966, two days before a quake, rattlesnakes invaded the town of Parkfield, California.

The site of several critical fault lines, California has offered some other recent evidence of animal sensitivity to tremors. James Berkland is a geologist in the San Francisco area who relies on highly unusual data to back up his earthquake predictions: He tracks the number of missing pets that are reported in the classified advertisments of local newspapers. Berkland is convinced that animals respond to currents generated in the earth's electromagnetic field. In his view, changes in that field are triggered by erratic pres-

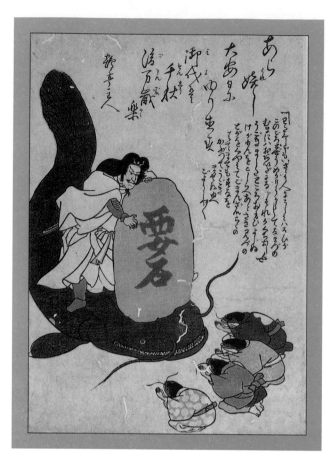

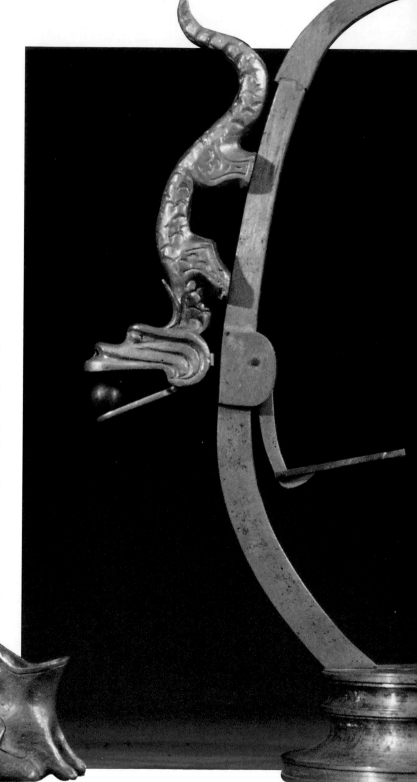

To calm tremors in the earth above, a nature god subdues a giant catfish before a kimonoed audience of smaller fish in this old Japanese print. Modern studies have revealed that catfish swim erratically just before an earthquake, perhaps because they sense minute disturbances in the earth's electromagnetic field.

sures along a fault line in the days leading up to a quake, and these are enough to upset animals to the point that they wander off and get lost. By monitoring the flow of lost animals, Berkland hopes to detect any significant increases that might signal earthquake activity.

James Berkland also keeps an eye on the tidal patterns along the California coast. He believes that the enormous energy released by the pounding of waves on the shoreline may contribute to the unstable condition that exists along the fault lines. When his two indicators coincide—when there is an upswing in the number of missing pets and abnormally high tides—Berkland will predict that seismic trouble is brewing.

Many scientists dispute Berkland's theories, and his unconventional techniques have caused controversy. Yet he insists that over a period of fifteen years during the 1970s and 1980s his predictions of earthquakes were accurate 75 percent of the time. Perhaps the most impressive verification of his theory was seen in the autumn of 1989, when a high incidence of lost pets coincided with especially high tides along the Pacific coastlines. Berkland predicted that a major earthquake would occur in the San Francisco Bay Area during the week following October 14. True

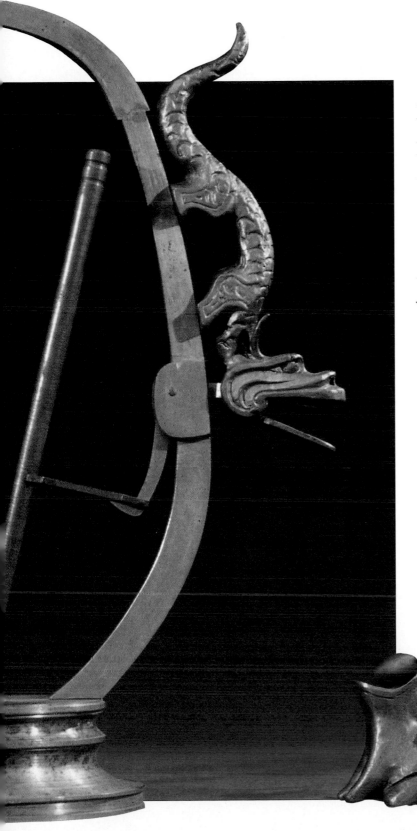

Once deemed the cause of earthquakes, dragons now serve as quake detectors in this replica of a second-century Chinese seismograph. When a tremor jars the device, a rod tips toward the quake's point of origin; this opens the jaw of the dragon nearer the epicenter and releases a ball into the mouth of a waiting toad. In China, earthquakes are thought to presage political upheaval—a belief eerily reinforced in 1976, when a devastating quake struck six weeks before the death of Mao Zedong.

to his warning, on October 17, while baseball fans the world over were awaiting the beginning of a World Series game, the Loma Prieta fault near the city of Santa Cruz shifted dramatically, resulting in an earthquake that killed sixty-seven people and caused widespread property damage.

There are several possible explanations for the reputed ability of animals to detect changing currents in the earth's electromagnetic field. In the brains of bees and pigeons, for example, there are trace quantities of magnetite, a magnetic ore, that apparently acts as a kind of internal compass in helping them navigate as they fly. Another possibility is that animals have some type of sensory device, not yet understood by biologists, that allows them to detect the clouds of electrically charged ions that are believed to flow away from the earth prior to an earthquake.

Some researchers believe that humans as well as animals can respond to this sort of electromagnetic energy under certain conditions. Scientist James Beal contends that variations in the earth's magnetic field can trigger responses in the nervous systems of certain people who are particularly sensitive to such anomalies because of quirks in their body chemistry. Beal suggests that the religious leaders and shamans of the past may have been unknowingly responding to such input as they made their decisions about where to situate temples and omphalos stones.

A British archaeologist named Francis Hitching has offered an alternative explanation for human sensitivity to the forces hidden within the earth. He points out that certain kinds of rock, particularly crystals such as quartz, are piezoelectric—that is, they give off a measurable electrical charge when they are subjected to pressure. Hitching

Bathers take the waters at Baia, a Roman spa town north of Naples, in this picture from a thirteenth-century travel guide. Each spring listed in the book supposedly had distinct healing powers. This one, good for the stomach, also "lifted souls and sent away sighs."

ments after this man climbed onto the chimney, the whole pile of rocks collapsed and fell down the slope.

Luckily, the other climber was not seriously injured, but LaChapelle was left utterly mystified. She wondered if her inability to tackle the chimney was instinct, pure and simple, or the result of some sort of nonverbal warning from the rock. Years later, LaChapelle still considers the latter a possibility, and she has decided that Hitching's theory may provide the scientific explanation. If the rocks that formed the dangerous chimney had been under destabilizing pressures, it is possible that they may have accumulated enough voltage to be detected by her body, even if she was not able to sense the problem at a conscious level. "What I do know," LaChapelle concluded, "is that one must be in tune with the rock and at ease with it from a great deal of climbing to feel it at all. The others were not as experienced rock climbers as I, and they felt nothing unusual until the rock slid out."

When Aristotle declared that air was one of the four fundamental elements, he did so purely out of respect for its essential nature: Without air, he reasoned, no one could live. He had no idea that air was a mix of many gases—mainly nitrogen and oxygen, but with minute quantities of argon and other gases as well. Like most people today, Aristotle simply took the air for granted: It was always there and largely unremarkable.

Another way of thinking about the atmosphere, however, is as a great ocean of air and water vapor, the latter existing in the form of clouds. Although 99 percent of the atmosphere's mass lies in the first 50 miles above sea level, traces of it have been detected some 18,000 miles above the earth. At the very bottom of this ocean of air is the earth's surface, on which everything is subjected to a more or less constant fifteen pounds of pressure per square inch. Any fluctuation in this pressure has its results: They can be serious ones, such as higher tides, or minor ones, such as stopped-up ears and three-minute eggs that take five minutes to cook.

All of the phenomena that are collectively referred to as the weather—winds, clouds, storms, rain, and the like—occur within the bottom five to ten miles of the atmosphere, a region that is known as the troposphere. An enormous amount of energy is gathered, exchanged, and released within this narrow band of the air ocean. Gentle breezes and thunderstorms, the vast sweep of trade winds and the potent jet streams at altitudes of 30,000 to 45,000 feet, lightning, hail, sleet, and snow are all expressions of the thermal, electrical, or rotational energy that flows continuously

notes that quartz is a constituent part of many different types of rock and therefore is extremely common. He speculates that quartz crystals, trapped within other rock formations and exposed to great pressure, may give off sufficient electrical current to draw a response from the human body.

There is no clear indication that anyone has ever been so sensitive to piezoelectric charges as to be able to anticipate earthquakes, but there is some intriguing evidence to suggest that the tiny electrical currents may weave their spell over mountaineers. It has long been observed that the very best climbers often forge an uncanny sense of oneness with the rocks they ascend. One veteran mountaineer named Dolores LaChapelle described a startling experience that befell her while climbing a challenging peak in Canada. Approaching a rock formation known as a chimney, she found that she could not bring herself to step onto it. After trying several times to raise her foot to make the easy first step, she asked another climber to assume the lead. Mo-

through the great recycling system of the atmosphere.

All of this activity has had a deep effect on the ways human beings view the world. The intricacies of weather are a constant source of interest, as Mark Twain noted more than a century ago. Oddly enough, however, most people today seem to assume that the weather is nearly as unpredictable now as it was in Twain's time. In fact, the science of meteorology has come a long way, particularly during the past thirty years. The United States and other nations now spend billions of dollars every year on weather forecasts, and the accuracy of the reports has steadily improved. A typical forty-eight-hour forecast is now correct about 80 percent of the time—a record twice as good as could be claimed in the 1960s.

In making their predictions, meteorologists for the National Weather Service in the United States depend upon a worldwide data-collecting network of satellites, ocean vessels, airplanes, and ground weather stations. Twice each day, readings on temperature, wind, precipitation, humidity, atmospheric pressure, and many other weather variables are received by the National Weather Service headquarters in Washington, D.C., and fed into some of the world's most powerful computers. The data can then be analyzed by the forecasters.

The science of weather prediction dates from the development in the 1700s of various meteorological instruments. The barometer, which measures changes in atmospheric pressure, was the most notable of the new tools. For

Eyes shaded by parasols, women lie buried to their chins in a hot "sand bath" in Beppu, Japan. Each year, millions of tourists visit Beppu for treatments ranging from the sand baths—said to relieve arthritis—to more conventional immersions in mineral springs.

thousands of years prior to these developments, however, people relied on less sophisticated methods for determining whether a day would be fair or foul. And many of the amateur forecasting methods developed in that time are still widely observed today.

Some people, for instance, swear that they can feel it in their bones when rain is coming. This is not an unlikely or illogical claim, because humidity can aggravate certain physical conditions such as arthritis. Birds figure prominently in other folkloric forecasting methods. Swallows are said to swoop close to the ground before a rain; seagulls will congregate and sit out a rainstorm together. Geese and other migrating birds show the tendency to fly higher in fair weather than in foul.

The popular aphorism "red sky at night, sailors' delight" may be the distillation of centuries of amateur weather observation, but it holds up well under scientific scrutiny. In the northern temperate zone, most weather systems move from west to east because of the earth's rotation. Dry air tends to reflect the red component of the sunlight filtering through it, and moist air accentuates the yellow end of the spectrum. Therefore, a red sky at sunset is a good indication that there is dry air—and fine weather—on its way in from the west.

Other bits of weather folklore are less serviceable. There seems to be little validity to the old saw that reclining cows indicate rain or that spiders leave their webs when rain is approaching or that dark breastbones in the Thanksgiving Day turkeys bespeak a hard winter to come. Nor does the groundhog's shadow on the second day of February seem to have much to do with anything other than the weather on that particular day. One traditional weather predictor that does appear to hold water concerns the woolly bear's stripes. Many countryfolk swear by the certainty that the wider the fuzzy caterpillar's brown middle stripe, the milder the winter will be. Scientists have found no evidence to validate this homely long-range forecasting technique, but they admit that it seems to be accurate more often than not.

When meteorologists talk about weather, they are referring to short-term fluctuations in the atmosphere over a number of hours, days, or weeks. The broader term "climate" refers to the atmospheric conditions of a region over a long period. Changes in climate that take millions of years to transpire have profoundly affected life on earth. The planet has undergone a more or less regular cycle of ice ages alternating with warmer interglacial periods. Evidence from plant fossils and rocks scraped by glaciers as they creep across the land indicates that the earth has experienced three major ice ages in the last 600 million years. At the height of the last ice age, which lasted three million years and ended in about 8000 BC, glaciers covered much of the northern hemisphere. They extended as far south as present-day St. Louis and New York City and smothered the land under mile-thick sheets of ice.

The advances and retreats of glaciers altered the landscape of several continents in significant ways. In North America, for example, the ice scooped out the basins of the Great Lakes and bulldozed vast quantities of sand and soil to form Long Island in New York. In addition to such direct effects on the shape of the land, glaciers changed the conditions for life on the planet by trapping enormous quantities of water in ice. This lowered the levels of the seas and reduced the amount of rainfall in the tropics. During the last ice age, a drop in the level of the Bering Sea created a land bridge between Siberia and Alaska, allowing humans to cross from Asia into the Americas.

The exact reason for ice ages periodically gripping the earth is far from certain. Glacial cycles are probably influenced by wobbles in the earth's rotation, which change the angle at which the sun's rays strike the planet. Another possible contributing factor may be variations in the earth's orbit, which cause the planet to swing farther away from the sun. Even minor changes in the amount of solar energy reaching the earth are enough to alter climate patterns. Scientists believe that the enormously slow, but steady, drifting of the continents has also had an effect. As the continents gradually move, they cause alterations in the flow of

Energy Points in Red Rock Country

For people with psychic powers, writes New Age lecturer Dick Sutphen, the world is dotted with "positive or negative power spot[s] where a great concentration of energy emits from the earth." He calls these places vortices and suggests that they exist in Stonehenge and the Bermuda Triangle. Even more powerful, Sutphen contends, is the red-rock country near Sedona, Arizona. There, he and other psychics have identified four separate vortices: Boynton Canyon *(below, left),* Cathedral Rock *(below, right),* Bell Rock, and a site called Airport Mesa, near the town's small landing strip.

Situated in a region held sacred by the Yavapai Indians, Sedona has inspired a wave of New Age pilgrims. On the occasion of the so-called Harmonic Convergence, for example, in August 1987, five thousand visitors flocked to the area. Many of the modern-day seekers report that they experience strange physical sensations. Hot hands and feet are oft-heard claims, along with relief from fatigue. Other visitors allege a range of paranormal experiences: telepathy, automatic writing, memories of past lives, precognition, visions, healings, and UFO sightings.

According to some reports, even the town's arts community is benefiting from the vortices. The region's energy, says one gallery owner, "can only be used in a positive way." Those who try to create something negative, he says, "don't stay around. . . . The red rocks spit them right out of here."

A full moon rises behind the rugged sandstone spires of Cathedral Rock (above), supposedly intensifying the area's already potent psychic energy. At left, a rock "energy circle" in the shape of an Indian medicine wheel has been put in place by New Age enthusiasts to surround a point in Boynton Canyon that they consider to be the most powerful of Sedona's vortices.

ocean currents that carry warm equatorial waters toward the North and South poles.

Since the last ice age ended 10,000 years ago, at least one long period of exceptionally low temperatures has interrupted the current interglacial period. In the seventeenth century, Europe endured a succession of severely cold winters and chilly summers that froze the Dutch canals, ruined the grape harvests in France, and brought crop failure and famine to Russia and as far east as China. This cooling trend lingered throughout much of the following century and may have been responsible for the devastatingly cold winters of the American Revolution, when Washington's troops suffered through their brutal encampment at Valley Forge and armies trundled cannons across the frozen surface of Long Island Sound. Climate historians have linked the prolonged chill of this so-called Little Ice Age to a temporary decline in the sun's energy output. The dark smudges on the solar surface called sunspots, whose numbers wax and wane in cycles, were notably absent during much of this period.

The Little Ice Age is a forbidding reminder that, even during relatively benign periods like the one that human beings have enjoyed for the last 10,000 years or so, climate is never truly stable. There is strong evidence, for instance, that a small colony established by the Vikings in Greenland during the tenth century was wiped out by 1500 because of a change in the climate of that region.

The prospect of such a fate befalling future generations in other parts of the world cannot be dismissed. Since the dawn of the Industrial Revolution two centuries ago, the burning of coal and oil has pumped billions of tons of carbon dioxide into the earth's atmosphere. Atmospheric CO_2 traps solar heat reflecting back from the earth, causing a gradual elevation in temperature. Many climatologists believe that this so-called greenhouse effect has raised world temperatures one degree Fahrenheit since 1900—and they expect the trend to accelerate. Although the projections made by scientists exploring this problem are highly specu-

lative at this point, there is the possibility that earth temperatures a century from now could be nearly ten degrees higher on average than the temperatures today. The results of such a change would include devastating heat waves, long droughts, and a rise in the levels of the oceans. This last effect would be caused by the expansion of seawater— which increases in volume as it warms—and a partial melting of the polar icecaps.

If the air and the atmosphere have come to symbolize the potential dangers lurking in the future, the third Aristotelian element—fire—was the one that people in past ages most closely associated with danger. Fire was the lightning bolt cast down by the gods and the angry threat of the erupting volcano. It was a fierce weapon of war and the final affront of the pillaging barbarian conqueror. But fire could also be a positive symbol of comfort and good. It was the reassuring blaze inside the hearth and the chimerical light of the aurora borealis.

All life depends on the vast flow of energy that streams from the enormous fireball known as the sun. Solar energy warms the earth and nurtures the plants on which all animals ultimately depend. The light and heat that come from the sun are products of an ongoing process of nuclear fusion in which hydrogen is converted to helium under immense pressure at the center of the star.

The more familiar form of fire occurring on earth, the kind seen in the flaring of a match or in the blue spikes of a stove burner, is the product of a chemical reaction—the rapid joining of oxygen with other substances. Oxygen atoms combine particularly well with atoms of hydrogen and carbon, and these are the chief ingredients of such common fuels as coal, gasoline, natural gas, and wood. The chemical reaction gives off heat and light, along with such byproducts as soot (unconsumed carbon) and smoke (a combination of water vapor, carbon dioxide, and soot). The technical term for this process is combustion, a word that carries connotations of the explosive forces involved.

Learning to control and make use of fire was as important to the development of human society as the invention of tools and language. It provided protection from predators and made humans better hunters. Among other tactics, early hunters learned to set grass fires to drive game into traps for easy slaughter. Fire was one of the weapons the early cave dwellers used to claim their homes from the wild animals that might otherwise have occupied them. The warmth and light of hearth fires then made the caves livable. Some caves show evidence of continuous human habitation for 50,000 years or more. And anthropologists believe that the behavioral routines of cooking and eating in groups around fires must have encouraged oral communication among the early hunter-gatherers and thus contributed to the development of language.

Anyone who has ever sat around a campfire and shivered to the telling of ghost stories can appreciate the important role that fire must have played in humankind's earliest rituals of magic and religion. Shamans and priests would certainly have used fire to help create the appropriate mood for their ceremonies, and fire continues to play a part in all but the most austere religions today. Candles burn on the altars of most Christian churches, and Roman Catholics light candles for the souls of their deceased loved ones. Jews celebrate the festival of Hanukkah by ritually lighting the nine candles of a menorah.

Ritual fire has long found its way into civil affairs as well. In imperial Rome, the fortunes of the state were believed to depend upon a sacred flame that flickered inside the temple of Vesta, goddess of the hearth. The French saw fit to light a perpetual flame under the Arc de Triomphe in Paris to commemorate the Allied dead from the two world wars. And in Virginia's Arlington National Cemetery, a similar torch burns at the grave of slain President John Fitzgerald Kennedy.

All of these ritual uses of fire, along with numerous functional applications in cooking, providing warmth, powering industry, and waging war, are examples of ways in which humans have learned to domesticate fire and exploit the energy released by combustion. Two awe-inspiring natural sources of this energy—volcanoes and lightning—have never been brought under human control and, as a result, have maintained a fascination widely reflected in mythology and folklore.

Nearly everywhere that volcanoes are found on earth, they have evoked myths about the gods. The name of these unpredictable and destructive mountains is derived from Vulcan, the Roman deity associated with fire. The Hawaiians, whose islands contain some of the most active volcanoes in the world, spun out an elaborate web of mythology around Pele, their temperamental goddess of fire. She was said to unleash torrents of lava whenever she was angry with her subjects, and simply by stamping her foot, she brought on the earthquakes that often accompanied volcanic activity. In 1881, when Hawaii's largest volcano, Mauna Kea, erupted and threatened to envelop the town of Hilo in a river of lava, a princess of the royal family was quickly brought to the scene. The princess chanted prayers before the lava and made offerings of silk scarves and a bottle of brandy. According to island tradition, Pele was satisfied with these gifts, stopping the lava short of the town and quieting Mauna Kea.

There is some evidence that the Hawaiians living in prehistoric times may have gone to even greater lengths to appease their volcanoes, offering human beings as sacrificial victims. Similar practices may have been adopted in Central America, Java, and Africa as well. Given the capriciousness of volcanoes and their awesome destructive power, such drastic methods of pacification are perhaps not entirely surprising.

Worldwide, the scientists who study volcanic activity count some 600 active peaks and 10,000 dormant or extinct ones. These categories must be considered somewhat arbitrary, however, since supposedly quiescent volcanoes have been known to return angrily to life. Italy's Mount Vesuvius lay dormant for centuries until it blew sky-high in AD 79, ejecting a cloud of volcanic ash that buried Pompeii and two other towns at its base. After that, Vesuvius erupted at least once a century for the next thousand years. It then shut down for 600 years before exploding again in 1632, and the mountain has been active ever since.

The eruption of Mount Vesuvius was barely a pop compared with the blasts of two Indonesian volcanoes in the nineteenth century. In 1815, the explosion of Tambora ejected so much ash—an estimated thirty-eight cubic miles of the stuff—that it blackened the sky for three days. Lifted into the atmosphere and carried on the jet stream, the ash blocked enough sunlight to lower temperatures worldwide for several years to come. Farmers in the United States suffered frosts in July and remembered 1815 darkly as "the year without a summer." Sixty-eight years after Tambora's mighty detonation, the volcanic island of Krakatau went up in a blast that could be heard 2,100 miles away. The earth-

quake that accompanied the Krakatau eruption unleashed a tidal wave that killed 36,000 people on the nearby islands of Java and Sumatra.

The Indonesian islands are part of a vast ring of coastland and Pacific Ocean seabed in which the earth's crust is especially thin or stressed. This weakness allows magma from the underlying mantle of the earth to break through in places to the surface. Volcanoes form a line along the western rim of the Pacific Ocean, whereas the eastern rim is made up in part by the fault-ridden and earthquake-prone coasts of California and Alaska. The volcanically formed Hawaiian Islands are actually situated in the middle of a tectonic plate, but they are lying over what geologists call a hot spot, where magma from the mantle has forced its way through the crust.

Wary of the precipice, a Javanese villager dribbles orange soda into the steaming crater of Mount Bromo (below), one of the sixteen active volcanoes on his island. Local residents hope that such gifts—which may also include money, flowers, and food (right)—will keep the sleeping mountain god from stirring. During eruptions, they may return to the crater's rim with additional offerings, risking their lives to quiet the god.

In the Atlantic, the volcanically hyperactive islands of Iceland sit atop the Mid-Atlantic Ridge, along the seam between two plates. Icelanders have capitalized on one of the only concrete benefits of living in a volcanically active region—geothermal springs warmed by the subterranean heat of volcanoes. They are able to use the heat of these springs to warm their homes and generate electricity. New Zealand, Japan, and a few other nations that are situated in volcanically active regions of the Pacific have succeeded in doing the same.

While Vulcan's earthy fireworks have offered a few such advantages along with their unmatched capacity for devastation, lightning has cast its share of fear and fascination without such compensatory blessings. Lightning usually appears in association with thunderstorms, one of the atmosphere's most profligate outbursts of energy, whose spectacle can be both terrifying and wonderful. Jane Goodall, the famous researcher of chimpanzee behavior, has observed wild chimps at the height of a thunderstorm break into spontaneous displays of hooting, barking, and running. The violence of thunderstorms undoubtedly evoked a similar response in the earliest humans, and subsequent trappings of civilization have done little to repress our fear—with good reason.

Meteorologists estimate that, worldwide, 16 million thunderstorms occur every year and that there are two to six thousand such storms in progress at any given moment. The maximum current in a bolt of lightning is about 20,000 amperes, but all of the electrical energy in the estimated two billion bolts that transpire each year is wasted. In the United States, lightning claims an average of 400 human lives per year. Still, three out of four people hit by lightning survive, sometimes with severe burns but often without a scratch. Although lightning has the power to shatter trees or blow the nails out of a roof, its effects are strangely unpredictable. It has been known to tear the clothes off people without harming a hair, and—in at least one case—it has restored the sight of a blind man.

Scientists know that lightning is electricity generated by the violent churning of wind, rain, and hail inside a thundercloud. The connection between lightning and electricity was first demonstrated in 1752—in France by Thomas-François D'Alibard, who observed a spark jump from the base of a metal pole during a thunderstorm, and in America by Benjamin Franklin, who performed his famous experiment with the kite in that same year.

Occasionally lightning will take a form other than the familiar jagged streaks crackling down from the clouds to the earth. Bead lightning appears in bolts that seem to break apart into strings of disconnected flashes. A will-o'-the-wisp, on the other hand, is an ephemeral blue flame that seems to hover over a swamp. St. Elmo's Fire is another ghostly form of lightning, which appears on the masts and yards of sailing ships or on the wings of airplanes flying through storms. It consists of a ball or plume of bluish light that is the visible manifestation of an electrical charge concentrated on a point or along the narrow edge of a metal surface.

Ball lightning is a truly mysterious phenomenon. Unlike St. Elmo's Fire, it is not attached to its point of discharge. It generally manifests itself in the form of mobile, luminous spheres that travel across the sky or close to the ground, along telephone wires and fences. Ball lightning usually lasts no more than a few seconds, disappearing either with an explosive pop or with an eerie silence. It is sometimes destructive, but it has also been known to pass right through solid objects without leaving a trace. The re-

ality of ball lightning is well documented, but it has never been satisfactorily explained by scientists.

The most spectacular display of fire in the sky is undoubtedly the aurora borealis, also called the northern lights. These shimmering curtains of evanescent red and blue appear in winter, usually in the vicinity of the Arctic Circle but occasionally as far south as London or New York. The northern lights are triggered by high-energy particles streaming from the sun. The particles smash into atoms of earthly materials in the upper atmosphere, dislodging electrons. The energy generated in these collisions is expended in the form of light.

As far and away the most abundant substance on earth, water could hardly have been omitted from Aristotle's grand scheme of elements. Like earth, air, and fire, it too is a blend of some of the atmosphere's basic components— two molecules of hydrogen to one of oxygen. But with its uniform texture and dependable behavior, water has traditionally been thought of as the purest element of all. In the seventeenth century, the Belgian alchemist Jan Baptista van Helmont called water the *prima materia,* the fundamental matter that gave rise to all else on earth. The view of water as giver of life has been a consistent thread in the beliefs of many different cultures.

Three-quarters of the globe is covered by water, principally the salt water of oceans. The Pacific Ocean alone covers an area larger than all of the planet's landmasses combined. Of the 3 percent of the planet's water that is fresh rather than salty, only a quarter of that amount is in liquid form. The remaining 75 percent is locked up in glaciers and the polar icecaps. Nevertheless, the small percentage of fresh water that is not frozen fills enough springs, wells, streams, rivers, and underground reservoirs to nourish all the life on the planet.

Almost all surface water eventually finds its way to the sea, but an equal amount must somehow find its way back to the earth. More than 2,000 years ago, the anonymous author of the biblical Book of Ecclesiastes appeared to un-

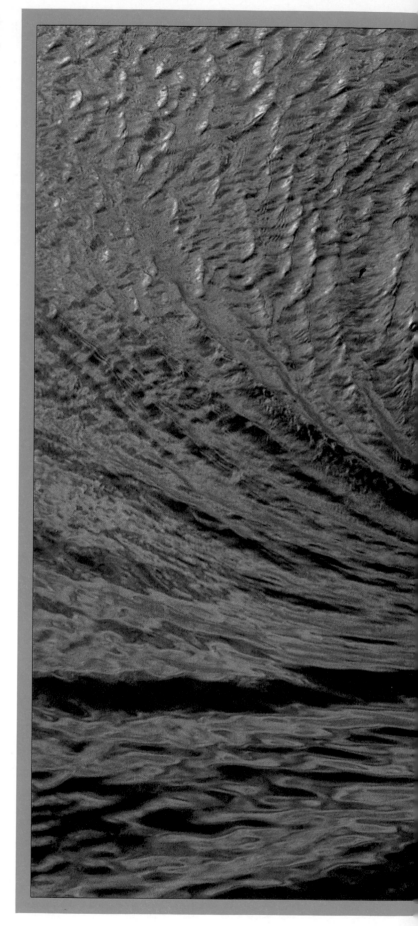

derstand this cycle intuitively: "All the rivers run into the sea; yet the sea is not full; unto the place from whence the rivers come, thither they return again."

How the cycle actually stayed in balance, however, remained a profound mystery for many centuries. The first puzzle for early natural philosophers was why the oceans never overflowed with all the world's rivers pouring into them. One hypothesis was that seawater was driven underground by giant whirlpools before surfacing again as rivers. But this only led to a second thorny question: How could the waters found on earth be fresh if all the oceans that were their sources were salty?

Not until the late eighteenth century was it widely understood that rain is the answer to both questions. Seawater evaporates into the atmosphere and leaves its salts behind, just as water is distilled when it boils and condenses in a laboratory retort. When the moisture from the seas falls again to earth as rain, it replenishes the ground-water system and eventually reappears in springs, wells, and rivers. Many observers have likened the everlasting flow of earth's hydrologic cycle to that of the human bloodstream, which also has no beginning and no end.

Most scientists agree that life on earth almost certainly originated in water, perhaps in tidal pools that provided a warm environment where amino acids could link together to form complex chains of proteins. Such a process may have occurred about 3.6 billion years ago, but another 3.2 billion years would elapse before the amphibians that were the most distant ancestors of the human race crawled from the tidal ooze to establish hegemony on the land.

Ancient peoples looked upon the oceans with a mixture of reverence and fear. The Babylonians, who lived along the Tigris and Euphrates rivers, in what is now the country of Iraq, regarded the ocean as a "home of wisdom" and believed that their sea god, Oannes, stepped forth from the Persian Gulf to bring culture, writing, and astrology to the human race. The Greeks, on the other hand, looked on the ocean as an unpredictable and treacherous adversary, whose qualities were personified by their sea god, Posei-

don. Every sailor feared the wrath of this capricious deity, who could with a wave of his trident turn a glassy sea into a storm-wracked nightmare of howling winds and crashing waves. In keeping with his destructive nature, Poseidon was also feared as the god who punished with earthquakes.

Rivers, like the oceans to which they flow, have been symbolized as powerful givers and takers of life. Almost all of the great early civilizations were nourished by rivers, and the people of those cultures worshiped gods who controlled the benificent flow of the great streams. Yet the floods that allowed these civilizations to thrive by distributing nutrient-rich silt over their farmlands could also be terribly destructive. So, many cultures endowed their rivers with harmful spirits as well.

The magnitude of the power attributed to rivers was reflected most dramatically in the legend, common to many cultures, of a great flood in which massive destruction was followed by regeneration. The biblical story of Noah is the best-known version of this tale, but biblical scholars believe that basic themes contained in this scriptural account may have been adapted from a similar legend passed on by the Sumerians. The Greeks had their own story of an epochal flood: In their version, the god Zeus becomes disgusted with the wicked ways of humanity and decides to put an end to the mortal realm by causing a mighty deluge. The Noah figure in the Greek myth is Deukalion, a son of Prometheus. Flood stories also find a place in the mythologies of Wales, Lithuania, Norway, Iran, Central America, Australia, and China.

Raft-borne scientists (opposite) dredge an ancient sinkhole near the Mayan ruins of Chichén Itzá in this aerial photograph taken in 1961. Mayan priests hurled living women and children into the pool, beseeching the gods for rain.

There are legends passed down in many North American Indian tribes that also tell of a great flood, but scholars who have studied this aspect of Indian lore suspect that the tales may have drawn heavily from early missionary accounts of Noah, which then spread from tribe to tribe. It is possible, however, that some of the Native American flood myths stemmed from an event that actually occurred at the end of the last ice age, some 10,000 years ago. Judging by geologic evidence, a natural ice dam melted and emptied the contents of a huge lake across much of what is now eastern Washington State.

Stupendous natural disasters may have spawned other flood tales, too. The Sumerian account on which Noah's story was based could have stemmed from a flood that ravaged much of the Tigris and Euphrates Valley in approximately 2800 BC. Similarly, the flood myth of Deukalion was, according to some scholars, based on a devastating tidal wave, or tsunami, that was caused by the explosion in about 1500 BC of a volcano on the Aegean island of Santorin. According to this theory, Santorin's wave washed over the island of Crete and accounted for the sudden collapse of the Minoan culture there. And with the Minoan influence suddenly in decline, the Mycenaean civilization came into its own on the Greek mainland.

The epic cleansing of the earth and subsequent rebirth of mankind, as portrayed in many of the flood myths, is echoed on a personal level in the sacrament of baptism. The worshiper who submits to this ritual initiation dies symbolically and is reborn in spirit. Although it is associated mainly with Christian-

Littered with latter-day spirit offerings, this holy well in Ireland's County Clare is known for the cure of toothaches, but it is also said to improve fertility and promote general good health.

ity, baptism was also a custom of the ancient Hebrews. The Old Testament prophet Ezekiel wrote: "I will pour upon you clean water and you shall be cleansed."

Among the Greeks, one of the most sacred ceremonies in the cult of the fertility goddess Aphrodite was a ritualistic bathing of her statue. The practice was carried over into Christianity in the veneration of the Virgin Mary, whose worshipers washed her icons in times of drought, beseeching the Blessed Mother to send rain. This custom reflects the seemingly timeless association of water with fertility. In the Sumerian alphabet, the letter A could in various different contexts mean water, sperm, conception, or generation. In the creation myth of the Pima Indians of New Mexico, a drop of rain falling on mother earth was sufficient to make her pregnant. Buddhists, too, have long celebrated the purifying effects of water. Many Buddhist temples were built over sacred springs so that worshipers could bathe before embarking upon their prayers.

In Western Europe a longstanding tradition attributes curative powers to sacred springs. Among the Greeks, for example, the custom of taking the waters to restore one's health dates back at least 2,500 years. In various parts of Britain, as well, there were holy wells long before the Christian era. The pagan inhabitants of the British Isles considered such springs to be gifts of the earth goddess. The same sites were usually given sanction by the Church and revered for their reputed ability to cure any ailment from warts to whooping cough.

Undoubtedly the most famous of the American legends regarding curative waters is that of the Spanish conquistador Juan Ponce de León. At the age of sixty-three, the great explorer set out through Florida on a futile search for a fabled fountain of youth. The limestone substrate found in the region does in fact support some of the largest and purest springs in the world. But as Ponce de León found out to his chagrin, none of the springs has the power to reverse the process of aging.

The use of therapeutic waters bubbling up from the earth has lost none of its appeal in modern times. Although medical researchers tend to scoff at the reputed curative powers of mineral waters, a few of these supposed drinking cures have some healthful benefits. By neutralizing stomach acids, for example, alkaline waters are fairly effective treatments against dyspepsia. Waters with high concentrations of Epsom salts are natural laxatives, and sufferers from anemia can benefit from drinking certain waters that are high in iron.

It is perhaps significant that the minerals and salts in these curative waters have been leached from the rocks and sediments of the earth itself—the first of Aristotle's ancient elements. Whatever the many blessings of water, the powers of fire, and the ubiquity of air, humankind's most inseparable bond has always been to mother earth herself. Although this bond was most tangibly felt in primitive human societies, its ties are still strong for those who believe they can sense them.

Carl Jung, who as a boy so thoroughly identified with the rock he discovered in his family garden, later in life reaffirmed his conviction that he could tap into the energy of the earth through its stones. In 1923, at the age of forty-eight, he began construction of a stone house at Bolligen in the north of Switzerland. Over the years Jung made additions to the building, using stones from a nearby quarry. Each room that he added answered a practical domestic need, but it also expressed a facet of himself that he wanted to represent in stone. He finally completed the building in 1955, after the death of his wife. The last addition was an upper story that, as Jung put it, "represents myself, or my ego-personality."

From the beginning, Jung understood that the house at Bolligen was to be a kind of maternal womb in which, as he wrote, "I could become what I was, what I am and will be." By the time the building was finished, it had become the psychiatrist's touchstone to his own life spirit. "It gave me," Jung recalled, "a feeling as if I were being reborn in stone." In doing so, perhaps, it allowed Jung's affinity for one of earth's elements to put him in contact with the spirit of the planet as a whole.

The Venerable Power of Trees

Centuries ago in France, pagan priests sacrificed other human beings to the trees they worshiped. As recently as the 1800s in Estonia, peasants festooned certain trees with wreaths and made offerings to them so that their cattle might thrive. Even today, Christian and Muslim pilgrims pay homage to an old, gnarled Arabian fig that is located just outside the city of Cairo; they seek cures for their ailments from the sacred tree, under which the Virgin Mary is said to have rested during her flight to Egypt.

For many early peoples, trees—especially those of great size, beauty, or apparent longevity—came to symbolize the wonders of creation and thus were revered as divine. Forests were thought to be the abodes of gods, and certain trees became associated with particular deities and were ascribed magical powers. As a means of appeasing the gods, worshipers laid offerings before the trees, prayed or meditated in the shelter of their branches, or tied ritual objects to them.

Some trees—including the Arabian fig and the bo tree, under which Gautama Buddha is said to have sought enlightenment—were sacred by virtue of their association with religious figures. Others were worshiped for their beneficence. In India, for instance, where the cool shade of wide-spreading trees is welcomed, banyans are protected by religious injunction. Examples of venerated trees, including some revered for their medicinal or alleged oracular powers, appear on the following pages.

A Gnarled Symbol of Peace and Redemption

One of the first trees ever cultivated, the long-lived olive is imbued with symbolism. According to legend, it sprang into being when Greek deities Poseidon and Athena were vying for possession of Attica. Aiming to please the other gods, Poseidon struck the earth with his trident to produce a horse. But Athena caused an olive tree to grow, and it was deemed the more valuable gift. Since ancient times, the tree has provided fruit for eating and oil for lamplight, cooking, and rituals.

The olive tree was also prominent in the Judeo-Christian tradition. The olive leaf the dove brought to Noah was a sign of redemption, and the garden of Gethsemane, where Christ took refuge before his arrest, was an olive grove. Medieval Christians believed the tree to be a safeguard against witches, and the olive branch has endured as a symbol of peace throughout history.

The Oak Tree: Fuel for Sacred Fires

Throughout Europe, the majestic oak was believed to embody the most powerful gods. Known in Scandinavia as the thunder tree, it represented Thor. In Greece it was dedicated to Zeus, who was allegedly born in its shelter. Greeks believed Zeus consecrated the forest of Dodona, endowing its oaks with the gift of prophecy. Jason's ship, *Argo,* was built of wood from Dodona, and the beams and masts warned the Argonauts of danger.

The oak symbolized fertility and good luck. Europe's Druids reportedly maintained perpetual oak fires; each year villagers rekindled their hearths from these sacred blazes, thought to bring fruitfulness and protection to the household. The tree's powers were trusted fervently. Saint Augustine, when trying to convert King Ethelbert, made his arguments under an oak tree lest he cast a spell on the superstitious ruler.

Home to Vishnu and Dispenser of Prophetic Dreams

There is a belief among Hindus that anyone who plants a useful tree attains punya, or "merit," and after death will spend 30,000 years in the heaven of Indra, then will achieve nirvana. The banyan, with its bizarre assemblage of aerial roots that grow from its branches down into the ground, is such a tree. Considered the dwelling place of gods—the Hindu deity Vishnu was said to have been born in the banyan's shade—the sacred tree symbolizes immortality, love, and protection. Some Indian women think the banyan promotes fertility; aphrodisiacs and medicines are concocted from its parts, and those who sleep beneath it are believed to experience prophetic dreams.

Providing Shade for Buddha's Enlightenment

Like the banyan, the bo tree is believed by Hindus to shelter their gods; it also represents the cosmic tree Asvattha, thought to shelter the world. The bo tree is sacred to Buddhists as well, for it was under such a tree that Buddha received enlightenment. To followers of Buddhism, the bo tree symbolizes creation, wisdom, and preparation for the afterlife. Destroying the tree is a sacrilege.

A cutting said to have come from Buddha's bo tree was transplanted to Anuradhapura, Ceylon, in 288 BC and is reputed to be the oldest existing tended tree. In 1948 the bo began to wither, and Buddhists flocked to resurrect it with gallons of milk, poured down its trunk. The tree was duly revived.

An Upside-Down Tree That Bears Many Gifts

Said by many to grow upside down because its skimpy branches resemble roots, the squat baobab tree thrives in much of Africa and in parts of Australia. The bountiful tree provides fruit for food, bark for rope and woven cloth, and medicinal powders for a variety of ailments. Some contend the baobab is magical: A drink of water in which the bark has been soaked is said to bestow strength. On the darker side, some Africans believe that the tree's white flowers are inhabited by spirits and that anyone who plucks the blossoms will be devoured by a lion.

Because the baobab's wood is soft and easily cut away, its massive trunk—which can be as much as thirty feet in diameter—is often hollowed to fill with water in the rainy season, enabling foraging tribes to survive on the parched land during dry months. Hollowed trunks are also used for shelter.

Ancient Sentinels Preserved by the Spirit of the Owl

Reaching heights of up to 370 feet, the redwoods of California and southern Oregon are the tallest trees in the world. With their cousins, the giant sequoias, they are the surviving members of a family of trees that may have originated more than 100 million years ago.

To the Native American tribes who lived among them, the redwoods were sacred, protected by the spirit of the owl. The Indians were reluctant to harm them, using only fallen wood and bark to make dwellings, canoes, baskets, and clothing. For two Indian tribes, the redwood fulfilled a spiritual purpose as well—to keep peace between them. According to legend, the Great Spirit instructed the two warring bands to sit beside a certain redwood and settle their differences. This they did, establishing the tree as a place of honor; thereafter tribe members paid tribute to the tree every time they passed it.

CHAPTER 3

A Green and Leafy Realm

Sometime in the year AD 63, according to a thirteenth-century chronicle, the evangelist Joseph of Arimathea sailed with eleven companions to the British Isles. Like other continental travelers of the day, he came first to the town in southwestern England now known as Glastonbury, which was a major center of the Cornish tin trade. Soon after his arrival, according to a centuries-old tradition still current in Glastonbury, Joseph climbed to the top of nearby Wearyall Hill and thrust his walking stick into the ground. The staff blossomed miraculously into a hawthorn tree—signifying, say pious commentators, the transforming power of the Christian faith.

Although its origin remains a matter of legend, an unusual hawthorn known as the Glastonbury Thorn has been a matter of historical record since the 1300s, when its likeness was included in the seal of Glastonbury Abbey. Whether or not Joseph planted the tree, the thorn was certainly no ordinary British hawthorn; botanists report that its modern descendants, grafted from cuttings of the original tree, are more like hawthorns found in the Middle East. Perhaps the best evidence of the thorn's uncanny origin is that—unlike ordinary hawthorns—the tree and its successors have almost always blossomed at Christmastime and then again near Easter. That oddly Christian schedule was first recorded in 1535, when a royal inspector sent a sample branch to the court of Henry VIII.

In the age of Puritanism that followed, miraculous trees fell out of favor. Religious zealots chopped down the oldest of the trees descended from the thorn, a double-trunked specimen high on Wearyall Hill. Local legend has it that the Elizabethan reformer who cut the first trunk was forced to halt his labors after a flying chip of wood blinded him in one eye. The second trunk then stood for fifty years until another Puritan returned to finish the task, apparently with no ill effects.

The Glastonbury Thorn was not put to rest so easily, however. By the time the Wearyall hawthorn died, avid gardeners throughout Britain and across the oceans had nurtured cuttings from the thorn into mature trees, most of which survived the Puritan reform. To this day, hawthorns grafted from the original Glastonbury stock flourish in the town itself and around the world, still faithfully flowering to mark the seasons of the Christian year.

Whether the trees of Glastonbury are a botanical fluke or an omen fraught with Christian power, their story is typical of the compelling roles that plants have played in human life and thought throughout history. Early hunter-gatherers lived in a kind of spiritual communion with plants, then as now a vital source of food, medicine, and other staples. Then, about 10,000 years ago, people discovered that certain crops could be deliberately cultivated, and human society underwent a very profound change. Footloose hunters became settled farmers, and new gods, cruel and variable as the weather or bountiful as the harvest, came to dominate human perceptions of the natural world.

In modern times, the emergence of science seemed at first to distance human beings from nature, stripping herbs, flowers, and trees of a long-accepted mystical significance. Yet in the end scientific research simply uncovered still greater human dependencies on the plant kingdom. By the eighteenth century, researchers had learned of the fundamental process of photosynthesis—a capacity unique to plant life—through which vegetation combines sunlight and carbon dioxide to create food and, as a byproduct, the oxygen we breathe. With the twentieth-century advent of artificial satellites, scientists found that plants form the very skin of the planet: a thin, green membrane with a surface area covering tens of millions of square miles. This skin covers not only fields and forests but also much of the mountains, and—in the form of green

and blue-green algae—the lakes and parts of the sea. Even the barest desert has a rugged form of plant life, its cacti and bone-dry weeds.

As they have since the beginning, plants also continue to fill a persistent, deeply human need that has little to do with simple physical survival. Whether the connection is as lighthearted as kissing under the mistletoe, as solemn as a funeral wreath, or as seemingly scientific as attempts to monitor the ''emotional'' response of plants to music or human thought, the link between humankind and growing plants seems likely to endure.

Of all the plants honored by the ancients, those most deeply venerated were the trees, from whose protective branches our primate ancestors emerged tens of millions of years ago. Tradition and archaeological evidence suggest that human beings have worshiped trees since the dawn of consciousness. On almost every continent, trees, rocks, and springs formed the sacred groves that were the earliest centers of spirituality. To their worshipers, stone stood for strength and permanence, and water for constant change and purification. Long-lived yet changing from season to season, trees represented a creative union of permanence and impermanence. They embodied growth, regeneration, and the cycle of life itself.

In fact, many of the very earliest known cultures considered the lives of certain trees to be at least as important as those of human beings. ''They say that primitive men led an unhappy life, for their superstition did not stop at animals but extended even

to plants," wrote the third-century Greek philosopher Porphyry. "For why should the slaughter of an ox or a sheep be a greater wrong than the felling of a fir or an oak, seeing that a soul is implanted in these trees also?"

Indeed, among peoples the world over, the felling of a tree was a serious business. In the ancient German forests, peeling the bark of a sacred tree was tantamount to murder, and the penalty was brutal: The perpetrator had his navel cut out and nailed to the tree. He was then forced to walk in circles around the tree until his intestines wrapped the trunk as a living replacement for the bark.

Many North American Indian tribes held similar beliefs. The Hidatsa, for example, regarded the giant cottonwoods of the Upper Missouri as sacred and harvested wood only from those that fell naturally. Then, in the twentieth century, younger Hidatsa began deliberately felling cottonwoods—a break with tradition to which their elders attributed every subsequent misfortune of the tribe.

As late as the 1920s, the Basoga of central Africa consulted local medicine men before cutting down any tree, lest the tree spirit become vengeful. If a medicine man granted his blessing, a member of the tribe would offer a bird and a goat as sacrifices to the tree spirit. Then, after his first ax blow, he would suck some sap from the cut in order to form a blood-brother relationship with the spirit.

Once the first human settlements arose, however, trees had to be felled to build and heat homes and to clear the fields. Inevitably, many such cultures came to think of tree spirits as somewhat mobile—and more forgiving. Trees were seen as dwelling places rather than as the permanent embodiments of the spirits themselves. A tree could be cut down, as long as the spirit within it was properly appeased.

At a desert stopping place, men of Australia's nomadic Arunta tribe erect a sacred pole called the Kauaua. The Arunta believe the Kauaua serves as a kind of portable tree that links this world to the realm of divinity. Their legends recount how the god Numbakulla climbed up the tree trunk and disappeared after creating the earth. So important is the Kauaua to the Arunta that a whole clan is said to have lain down and died when its pole was accidentally broken. They feared they had lost their connection to heaven.

Sir James Frazer, an early-twentieth-century compiler of folk practices and beliefs from around the world, recorded just such a custom in the islands of the Malay Archipelago. "When the Toboongkoos of Celebes are about to clear a piece of forest in order to plant rice," Frazer wrote, "they build a tiny house and furnish it with tiny clothes and some food and gold. Then they call together all the spirits of the wood, offer them the little house with its contents, and beseech them to quit the spot. After that they may safely cut down the wood without fearing to wound themselves in so doing."

On Wearyall Hill in Somerset, Hamish Miller tests the response of his dowsing tools near one of the famous Glastonbury hawthorns. Miller believes that the tree sits atop a potent channel of natural energy.

Yet even as the forests themselves began to fall, certain individual trees retained a fearsome power in the folklore of many regions. Until their conversion to Christianity at the end of the fourteenth century, for instance, Lithuanian villagers set aside special groves in which every branch and twig was sacred. Anyone who harmed a tree in such a grove would be sure to suffer death or accident at the hands of the site's spirit guardians.

Specific trees could also be linked to the fate of particular peoples or cities. According to the first-century historian Plutarch, the ancient Romans worshiped and fervently tended the fig tree of Romulus that stood in the Forum and a cornel tree, similar to a dogwood, that grew on nearby Palatine Hill. If either the fig or the cornel seemed ill or undernourished, members of the populace would run to the rescue with buckets of water, as if, wrote Plutarch, they were putting out a fire. Perhaps they feared that the death of

these trees would mean the end of their city as well.

In many cultures, individual citizens could find their fates linked irrevocably to those of particular trees. In ancient Rome and Palestine, for example, a family planted a sapling when a child was born; so long as the tree thrived, so did the child. Eastern Europeans planted pairs of trees outside the doors of newly married couples, hoping to ensure that the bride and groom would live together as peaceably as did the two trees.

Even healing rituals could lead to arboreal bonds. In one widely practiced European remedy for rickets in children, a young ash was split vertically and held apart while the afflicted child was passed through the split several times. Both tree and child were then tightly bound and tended carefully. It was thought that if the ash recovered, so would the child. If the tree died, the child would follow.

By the 1500s, yet another version of the personal tree appeared in Europe as nobles began planting ancestral oaks, elms, and other stately trees on their estates. Linked closely with the life and reputation of their aristocratic owner, such trees could be deliberately cut down by the state if their master turned traitor.

The mystical power of a tree depended in large part upon its species. In Europe, the lofty oak was the most re-

By hugging the tree at left, a woman and child act out their sense of spiritual kinship with other forms of life and protect the tree from a woodcutter's blade. The two are part of a growing, nonviolent movement in India that has set about trying to put an end to deforestation. The tactic of putting human bodies between trees and the loggers' tools was popularized by a group called Chipko, whose name is from the Hindu word meaning "to embrace."

vered of all trees. For reasons that scientists are still unable to fully explain, oaks are more likely than other trees to be struck by lightning, and so they were often associated with storm gods: the Greek Zeus, who wielded the lightning bolt; the Norse thunder god Thor; the Germanic Donar. Russians in the old city of Novgorod and their Lithuanian neighbors to the southwest would keep oak fires burning perpetually in honor of their sky gods, Perun and Perkunas. For their part, the Celtic priests known as Druids made human and animal sacrifices in oak groves in order to bring rain and thus fertility to the land.

A more ambiguous case was that of the apple tree, which was linked in Celtic tradition with paradise (Avalon, the name of a mystical British land, means "isle of apples") but also traditionally identified with the biblical fruit tree that fatally tempted Eve. In keeping with their mixed reputation, apples were employed both as remedies for various ailments and as ingredients in evil potions—an association that lingers today in the poisoned apple of the Snow White fairy tale.

If the apple tree's character was a mixture of good and evil, elder trees were generally considered wholly wicked, perhaps because of their twisted, deceptively human appearance. Folk wisdom held that witches frequently transformed themselves into these trees or simply dwelled in them. Skilled artisans never chose the wood of an elder when building a cradle, for fear that an angry witch would shake the cradle savagely or otherwise injure the child sleeping within. Similarly, it was thought that a beating with an elder stick would stunt a child's growth. The evil of the tree was even reflected in Christian legend: Judas Iscariot was said to have hanged himself from an elder after betraying Jesus Christ.

Above and beyond the ordinary trees of earth stood another kind of tree altogether: a vast religious symbol that cultural historians call a world tree or a cosmic tree. Found in many traditions, such a towering supernatural creation served as a vertical axis linking the heavens, the earth, and the underworld. In the Norse sagas, the mighty evergreen ash Yggdrasil was rooted in earth and held up heaven with its branches. Yggdrasil had three principal roots, one penetrating into Niflheim, the world of the dead, another into the land of snow and ice where giants lived, and a third into Midgard, the home of humankind. On the crown of the tree perched an eagle representing life and knowledge; at its base, the giant serpent Nidhögg and his brood gnawed constantly at the roots. A troublemaking squirrel, Ratatösk, ran up and down the trunk carrying taunts and threats from one inhabitant to the other.

According to the *Elder Edda* saga, the god Odin once hung himself, wounded, from the great tree in order to gain runic wisdom: "Nine whole nights on a wind-rocked tree / Wounded with a spear. / I was offered to Odin, myself to myself, / On that tree of which no man knows."

Guided by a ritual master, a Malagasy youth bows his head against a sacred tree, begging forgiveness for any offenses he may have given to the spirits of his ancestors. In Madagascar, spirits are believed to reside in trees, which are held in high esteem and symbolize the continuance of life.

Like the Norse gods themselves, Yggdrasil was fated to die on the day of Ragnarok, the final battle between good and evil. On that day, said the sagas, the serpent at its foot would at last gnaw through the root of the mighty ash. Then Yggdrasil would crumble and fall, taking the rest of the cosmos with it into eternal chaos.

The cosmic tree of the Hindu Upanishads, on the other hand, was an inverted bo tree named the Asvattha. It was described as having roots extending into the sky and branches covering the earth. Like Yggdrasil, the Asvattha had three main roots, but while those on the Norse tree represented three cosmic worlds, in the Hindu religion the roots signified three great gods: Brahma the Creator, Vishnu the Preserver, and Shiva the Destroyer. For the devout Hindu, however, even the cosmic tree stood in the way of enlightenment. According to the sacred Bhagavad-Gita, a religious seeker must renounce the Asvattha

In India, small human touches transform two sacred trees into living shrines: A votive mask tucked into the knothole below honors the cosmic life force embodied by trees; the tree opposite becomes the image of a deity with the addition of a bit of fabric and paint.

entirely, cut the tree at its roots, and "seek the place from which one never returns." Only then would the Hindu be able to transcend earthly understanding and become one with the universe.

Still other mythical trees have played narrower parts in the great drama of creation. In Judeo-Christian traditions, a tree of life is said to have grown inside the tree of knowledge, at the center of the primordial Garden of Eden.

As recounted in the biblical Book of Genesis, Adam and Eve sampled only the forbidden fruit of the tree of knowledge—the fruit that brought physical death and estrangement from God. Had the hapless couple also tasted the fruit of the tree of life, they would have been rendered immortal, and a common Jewish tradition adds that they would have gained a perfect understanding of the unity of life, death, and redemption. Instead, they and their descendants were driven from the garden forever.

The trees of Eden also figure in many early Christian legends. One medieval story recounted an episode in which Adam's son Seth returned to Eden to beg mercy for his father, who was dying. Seth was met at the gates by an archangel, who gave him three seeds taken from the tree of knowledge. The spirit told Seth to place the seeds on Adam's tongue. When Adam received the seeds, he laughed for the first time since his fall from grace, recognizing that human beings would one day be redeemed by means of the trees that would grow from those seeds.

According to the same tradition, saplings from the seeds were later transplanted to Jerusalem, where their three trunks intertwined into a single tree. Centuries later, wood from that tree was used to make the cross on which Jesus was crucified, and in fulfillment of the archangel's prophecy, at the crucifixion, Christ's blood fell to earth to redeem Adam and his descendants. Indeed, for many people the holy cross itself is yet another variant on the cosmic tree, a symbolic bridge between earth and heaven, humanity and the divine.

If trees are the most awe inspiring of plants, the vines and other vegetation that cling to their branches have often been next in order of reverence. In Europe, the best known of these arboreal parasites is the mistletoe, a deep green plant with gleaming white berries. Noted for its highly unusual habit of growing in treetops without touching the earth, mistletoe was especially revered by the Celtic Druids, because it favored their sacred oak.

According to the first-century Roman naturalist Pliny, harvesting mistletoe was a matter of solemn druidic ritual: A white-robed priest climbed the tree with a golden sickle to sever the parasite from the branch, and another Druid caught the sacred plant in a cloth before it was desecrated by contact with the earth. If all went well, the priests sacrificed two white bulls in thanks. The carefully gathered plant could then be used as a cure for a wide range of ailments and in fertility potions for both cattle and women. The association between mistletoe and fertility persists today in the well-loved Christmas custom of kissing under a sprig of the plant.

Well into the twentieth century, peasants from Italy to Sweden also gathered mistletoe—often by knocking it down with stones—as a protection against household fires, lightning strikes, and simple bad luck. Many believed that the seemingly heaven-sent plant was powerful enough to ward off the spells of witches and sorcerers, serving as a general antidote to all forms of evil.

Because mistletoe rarely fell spontaneously from its airy perch, it was also prescribed as a cure for the "falling sickness," or epilepsy. The medieval theory known as the doctrine of signatures applied a similar logic to many other healing herbs as well. According to this line of reasoning, which was generally accepted throughout Europe for centuries, a plant's medical powers could be deduced from its physical properties, or signature. For instance, aspens and poplars shiver in the slightest breeze, so they were thought to provide cures for fevers and agues. Because the willow grows in moist places, it was prescribed for rheumatism and other ailments thought to be brought on by dampness. Plants that resemble male or female genitals were believed

The TREE of the SOUL.

PARTLIGHT OF MAJESTIE

PARADISE

SOLAR WORLD

SPIRIT

to increase fertility and sexual desire.

The most potent botanical form of all was that of a human being. In Europe, the mandrake, an herb with a two-pronged root that resembles legs, has been sought for centuries as an ingredient in love potions. Carried close to the body, the root—itself called mandrake—was also thought to cure sterility in men and promote fertility in women. In the Book of Genesis, Jacob's wife Rachel bargains for mandrake to end her barrenness; not much later she bears Jacob a son. In yet another application of the root, the ancient Greeks, Romans, and Arabs used mandrake as a sleeping potion and anesthetic.

Despite the various beneficial effects that folk wisdom attributed to the mandrake, there was something about the plant's quasi-human shape that led to darker traditions. European lore had it that mandrake grew beneath the gallows on which murderers died; the stories also linked the root to the devil and the underworld. Witches, too, were believed to use mandrake roots in their spells. In many parts of medieval Europe, it was unwise for a woman to keep mandrake in her house for any reason; possession of the root could be cause enough for hanging or burning.

A widespread notion was that a mandrake root let out a ghastly shriek when pulled from the ground. Supposedly, hearing that cry could prove fatal or bring on insanity, a belief that explains why Shakespeare's young heroine Juliet feared the sound of "shrieks like mandrakes' torn out of the

97

The Sad Tale of Treaty Oak

In another place and time, Paul Stedman Cullen might have met the same fate he inflicted on his victim. Indeed, some Texans muttered half seriously about hanging the middle-aged drifter from a limb of Treaty Oak, the 600-year-old tree in an Austin city park that he deliberately poisoned with herbicide. As news of the peculiar tragedy spread in May of 1989, people grieved for the venerable tree. Under its boughs, legend suggests, Texas founding father Stephen F. Austin signed an Indian treaty.

As the effects of the poisoning grew more pronounced, people were shocked into recognition of the bond between humans and other living things. Get-well cards arrived from as far away as Japan and Australia, and well-wishing visitors deposited poems, flowers, and even chicken soup at the foot of the tree. A few people were so deeply moved that they fell to their knees and prayed beside the dying oak. Despite every effort, however, it became clear that nothing short of a miracle could save Treaty Oak.

Cullen's motives in attacking the tree remain a matter of conjecture. Police have mentioned a failed love affair and also the possibility that the attacker was carrying out some sort of occult ritual. Whatever his motivation, Paul Cullen was sentenced in May of 1990 to nine years in prison for his crime against nature.

earth, / That living mortals, hearing them, run mad." The danger was taken seriously enough that mandrake hunters often trained dogs to do the uprooting while their masters remained at a safe distance.

In the modern era, mandrake's supposed healing powers have fallen into disrepute, immeasurable by the techniques of medical science. More medically effective is another plant with a humanlike form—ginseng, from the Chinese words for "man" and "plant."

According to Chinese tradition, ginseng forms when lightning strikes a mountain stream. The energies of the lightning and the flowing water coalesce into a root and pass on to those who consume it. As long as the ginseng root remains underground, claims another legend, it becomes larger and more human in appearance every year. If it is left undisturbed for 300 years, the root emerges as a creature that looks like an ordinary human being but has pure white blood that can restore the dead to life. Provided such a being can elude human hunters anxious to collect its blood, it will eventually depart the earth to wander forever among the distant stars.

Whether or not they truly believe in spacefaring ginseng, traditional Chinese physicians have shown considerable faith in the efficacy of the root itself, which they have been prescribing for more than nineteen centuries as a universal cure and effective aphrodisiac. In an approach reminiscent of the European doctrine of signatures, doctors treat the ailments of various parts of the body with the corresponding portion of the ginseng root. The "head" of the ginseng is used for an aching or injured head, the legs for leg ailments, and so on.

Long ago, collecting ginseng was considered as dangerous as gathering mandrake, in part because of rampant banditry, in part because the root was thought to attract a protective guard of panthers and tigers. Some ginseng hunters even warned of a small demon that disguised itself as a ginseng root and slowly retreated into the forest to lure the unwary into danger. In sheer self-protection, ginseng hunters in China at one time joined forces to form a defensive society for the safe collection of the root. Each member was sworn to preserve the strictest moral character, for it was believed that ginseng would reveal itself only to the pure of heart.

Although the imperial family cultivated its own variety of ginseng, Chinese emperors paid ginseng hunters handsomely for wild roots, which were considered more potent. In gathering the ginseng, the collectors took great care to preserve even the tiniest rootlet. They would divert a stream to wash a single ginseng root out of the soil rather than allow its small hairs to get dried and broken by handling.

By the early eighteenth century, overgathering of wild Asian ginseng had sharply reduced the supply. (The Asian plant has since become all but extinct except in the remote Sikhote-Alin mountains along the Soviet coast of the Sea of Japan.) To ease the shortage, the Chinese turned to a plentiful, though less potent, type of ginseng found in the deciduous forests of North America. Called Little Man by the Cherokee, the root had long served as a medicine for several American Indian tribes. A Cherokee headache remedy, ginseng was also used as a life-saving cure by the Iroquois, the Creek, and the Chippewa tribes. The Pawnee employed it in love potions.

American ginseng was soon flowing to the Far East in large quantities. After a trip to Ohio in 1784, George Washington noted in his diary that "in passing over the mountains, I met numbers of persons and pack horses going in with ginseng." In 1788, Daniel Boone successfully prospected for ginseng in Kentucky, sending his treasure up the Ohio River for sale in Philadelphia. The well-known merchant John Jacob Astor

The hallucinogenic cactus called peyote inspires an annual 600-mile pilgrimage by Mexico's Huichol Indians. They collect the buds in reenactment of the gods' legendary quest for peyote.

also saw profit to be made in the business and by the early 1800s was exporting ginseng along with furs.

Today, as American businesses continue to ship wild and cultivated ginseng to the East, many in the West are themselves intrigued by the root, which researchers at Chelsea College in London have studied as a possible arthritis remedy. In the Soviet Union, ginseng is well accepted as a means of boosting stamina. Soviet scientists dose cosmonauts, mountain climbers, deep-sea divers, and soldiers with ginseng extract and a related plant called *eleutherococcus* to combat motion sickness, stress, and fatigue.

While ginseng is one of many herbs that are believed to heal ailments of the body, a small number of other plants—from coffee to the opium poppy—have long been known to have effects on the mind. Perhaps the most sinister of these organisms is a fungus known as ergot, an unobtrusive grain infection that strikes unexpectedly and with bewildering, often fatal effect.

Found on rye in damp weather or poor harvesting conditions, ergot can be beneficial in small quantities as an anesthetic. Medieval women used it to ease the pangs of childbirth. But when ergot-poisoned grain is baked in bread, a chemical component called ergotamine becomes lysergic acid diethylamide, or LSD. Those who eat the bread find themselves living in a world of hallucinations that are all the more terrifying because they appear without warning. As the blood vessels and nervous system are attacked by the poisoned bread, vividly realized demons and monsters accompany the victim's suffering. Those who survive may experience flashbacks as horrifying as the original episode for months afterward.

Skillfully carved, dressed in linen, and implanted with the hairlike sprouts of millet seeds, the root depicted in this peculiar engraving appears eerily human. Crafty peddlers passed off such creations as the coveted mandrake root, duping buyers who believed that human-looking plant roots carried magical powers.

According to a theory first advanced in 1976, ergotism may also have killed indirectly by causing the bizarre behavior of several young women in Salem, Massachusetts, in 1692. The Salem girls' fits and distempers, which one University of California researcher has linked to a possible case of ergot poisoning, led to a hysterical witch hunt and the execution for witchcraft of twenty-two presumably innocent villagers.

Across the continent, in the American Southwest, other hallucinogenic plants have long been accepted as a means of inducing mystical or religious experiences. Among the most commonly used are peyote "buttons" found at the head of the spineless peyote cactus. Amid solemn ceremony, celebrants eat the buttons and perceive colorful visions amid sensations of peace and happiness.

A Brulé Sioux legend from the 1920s relates that Grandfather Peyote first revealed himself to the Comanche nation through an old woman and her granddaughter who had become lost in the desert while seeking a cure for a tribal epidemic. Drawn mysteriously to a hidden peyote cactus, the two women drank its juice and immediately revived. The peyote then led them back to their tribe, where further applications of the plant cured the sick and dying. The sacred plant also gave them a kind of divine understanding, which they were able to pass on to other tribes.

Aztec rituals also included a number of plant hallucinogens, one of them a juice brewed from morning-glory seeds that contained a lysergic acid much like LSD. By drinking the sacred fluid, they believed, the Aztec priests could make contact with a host of savage gods. Another sacred Aztec plant, a psilocybin mushroom called *teonanactl,* or "flesh of God," supposedly helped priests become one with the divine.

Hallucinogenic plants figure in an ancient religious text, India's 3,000-year-old Rig Veda. According to this collection of hymns and prayers, the early Indo-Europeans worshiped and consumed an intoxicating plant juice called *soma* in rites that historians believe later developed into modern Hinduism. Soma's precise identity remains something of a pharmacological puzzle. Harvard researcher R. G. Wasson, a former reporter and banker who has made extensive studies of the ritual use of mushrooms by early cultures, argues that soma may well have been derived from *Amanita muscaria,* the fly agaric mushroom, a species that was also used by Siberian tribes during mind-altering religious rituals.

Whatever its true identity, soma evidently had an extraordinary effect on human perception. As recorded in the Rig Veda, the mysterious botanical fluid induced a state of exaltation verging on godhead. ''We have drunk Soma and become immortal; we have attained the light the Gods dis-

covered,'' reads one hymn from the ancient scripture. ''On all sides, Soma, thou art our life-giver: aim of all eyes, light-finder, come within us.''

For all the ancient glories of the soma, the mandrake, and the mistletoe, the primeval forest in which such plants thrived was in many ways an enemy to early civilization. Because it also served as a haven for outlaws and savage animals, the ancient woods posed a daunting barrier to farming, building, and free travel. As farmers gradually razed the first European forests, the prevailing view of wild plants and trees evolved from respectful coexistence to human domination. Even the study of plants was brought under firm intellectual control in the sixteenth and seventeenth centuries as Andrea Caesalpino in Italy and

Sporting a pyramid of greenery, a man impersonating Jack-in-the-Green cavorts during May Day festivities in this nineteenth-century painting. In British folklore, the sprightly Jack embodies the leafy spirit of spring.

Joseph Pitton de Tournefort in France separately categorized plants into thousands of precisely defined varieties.

Around the world, colonists saw "taming the wilderness" as the order of the day. To the seventeenth-century pilgrims of Plymouth Colony, the virgin forest was a "hideous and desolate wilderness . . . full of wild beasts and wild men." Back in Europe, fashionable gardeners took to trimming their plants and trees into geometric forms and fanciful shapes.

By the eighteenth century, the sheer volume of newly discovered plant and animal species inspired the Swedish naturalist Carl von Linné to

Covered head to toe with burrs from the burdock plant and crowned with a hat of flowers, a resident of Queensferry, Scotland, plays the part of the Burry Man—a magical fellow believed to bring luck.

term "haymaids." Under Linnaean rules it was reduced to the all but unpronounceable *Glechoma hederacea.*

Linnaean classifications also created something of a communications gap between the educated classes and countryfolk unfamiliar with the Latin tongue. Farmers found the new terminology unnatural and stultifying. Latinate plant descriptions were, as one British wag put it, "like writing an English grammar in Hebrew."

According to some historians of human thought, the greater price paid for this "scientization" of plants was the segregation of humans and plants into separate

develop a detailed system for categorizing plants. Writing under the Latin form of his name, Linnaeus, he became known as the father of modern botany—a development that hardly surprised his family, who had nicknamed him "the little botanist" when he was a boy of eight. In his book *Species Plantarum,* considered the bible of botanists to this day, Linnaeus baptized every known variety of plant with two Latin names, one for its genus and the other for its particular type or species.

The new system allowed traders, gardeners, and botanists from different regions to be sure they were talking about the same plants, but at a significant human cost. Inevitably, the Latin terms supplanted a time-honored vocabulary of local plant names ripe with meaning. In England, ground ivy once gloried in an array of folk names ranging from "catsfoot," "tun hoof," and "alehoof," to "Gill go by the ground," "Gill creep by the ground," and the peculiar

realms of existence. With the rise of science came a growing impatience with age-old beliefs in the religious or magical virtues of plants. To many a student of botanical lore, the natural world became a realm of dry, "lifeless" objects to be inspected and pigeonholed according to the latest scientific scheme.

But even as the botanists pondered their orderly classifications, other Westerners who felt sickened by the onslaught of industrialization developed a yearning for untouched nature. Between 1700 and 1850, the bulk of the European population was shifting from the countryside to the city, and small, individually farmed patches were consolidated into larger, more efficient tracts. From the perspective of new arrivals choking in smoke and homesick for green pastures, the city itself was a noisome wilderness, fraught with disease and danger, while the countryside was recalled as a haven of innocence.

A talented painter who gave up formal art training to pursue a scientific career, George Washington Carver attributed his remarkable agricultural discoveries to a mystical relationship with plants. "The secrets are in the plants," he once said. "To elicit them you have to love them enough."

Trees, meanwhile, had become more valuable with scarcity. As timber prices rose with the growth of shipbuilding and other industries, landowners began to plant trees as often as they cut them down. Trees also began to recapture some of their lost human significance. As early as 1691, one Thomas Tyron recorded that many believed "trees suffer pains when cut down, even as the beasts and animals do when they are killed."

By the nineteenth century, sensibilities about plants had come full circle. Referring to the neatly patterned order of a formal English garden, landscape artist John Constable said in 1822, "A gentleman's park is my aversion. It is not beauty because it is not nature." Instead, British poets such as William Wordsworth celebrated the beauty of natural scenes and wildflowers. In Wordsworth's poem "I wandered lonely as a cloud," the author comes upon "a crowd, a host, of golden daffodils; / Beside the lake, beneath the trees, fluttering and dancing in the breeze." Later just the memory of the flowers could lighten his thoughts: "And then my heart with pleasure fills, / And dances with the daffodils." The countryside even reassumed some of its religious significance: The American poet William Cullen Bryant called forests "God's first temples."

For his part, the nineteenth-century German poet Johann Wolfgang von Goethe believed he could communicate with the divine through the con-

templation of plants. The young man lay in bed at night visualizing the life cycle of a plant from seed to seed.

Eventually Goethe came to the conclusion that all plants derive from a single *Ur-plant,* a kind of ideal form. His notion that descendants of such an Ur-plant could adapt into new forms has been credited as a significant influence on Charles Darwin's groundbreaking theory of evolution.

Gradually the newly humanized view of plants spread into the study of botany itself. Among the best known of the researchers who combined technical expertise with a respect for plant life was the black American scientist George Washington Carver, whose lifework seemed to many to strike a near-perfect balance between employing plants to humanity's best advantage and revering them as marvelous creations of God.

A few decades after Goethe pondered his imaginary Ur-plant in cosmopolitan Europe, Carver was born into slavery in rural Missouri. Freed in early childhood by the American Civil War, as a young boy he spent most of his waking hours in the woods, where he would nurse ailing plants back to health in a hand-built greenhouse that he called his "garden hospital." Nicknamed "the plant doctor" by appreciative neighbors, the shy boy attributed his abilities to observations of the plants themselves. "All flowers talk to me," he said. "And so do hundreds of little living things in the woods. I learn what I know by watching and loving everything."

In 1891, Carver became the first black student to enroll at Iowa State University. After earning a bachelor's degree and then a master of science degree, he went on to accept a position as head of the newly formed agricultural department at Tuskegee, a black Alabama college founded by the ex-slave Booker T. Washington. During his first day at Tuskegee, Carver would later tell his students, he looked out of a window and experienced a vision, one of several divine revelations received throughout his lifetime. Instead of the barren clay of dirt-poor central Alabama, Carver said, he saw lush green hills dotted with prosperous, freshly painted farmhouses. From that day, the young professor took it upon himself to replenish the depleted soil of the South, which had been slowly leached of any nutrients by too many cotton crops.

Throughout the decades that followed, Carver's talents paid enormous dividends, as he found new and profitable uses for such previously unregarded crops as peanuts and sweet potatoes, plants that were all the more valuable because they helped to restore nutrients to the soil. As he had in childhood, Carver attributed his successes to the divine reality that he experienced through plants. Calling his laboratory "God's little workshop," the scientist prayed every day before entering it. "No books ever go into my laboratory," he told a New York audience. "I never have to grope for methods; the method is revealed at the moment I am inspired to create something new." He could do nothing, he said, without God to "draw aside the curtain."

By 1930, Carver not only had salvaged some of the South's endangered soil but had almost single-handedly created a quarter-billion-dollar regional agricultural industry. Despite generous offers of employment from such industrial titans as Thomas Edison and Henry Ford, he remained loyal to his work in Alabama. One day near the end of Carver's life, a visitor saw the famous agriculturalist gently caress a small flower on his laboratory bench. "When I touch that flower," Carver explained, "I am touching infinity. It existed long before there were human beings on this earth and will continue to exist for millions of years to come. Through the flower, I talk to the Infinite, which is only a silent force. This is not a physical contact. It is not in the earthquake, wind or fire. It is in the invisible world. It is that still small voice that calls up the fairies."

For Carver, that "fairy" voice belonged more to the divine force that pervaded all living things than to any particular plant. In recent decades, however, other students of botanical life have taken the notion of individual plant consciousness far more literally. Certainly, there are some types of plants that seem to act with eerie intentionality. The carnivorous Venus flytrap captures and eats helpless insects,

Tapping the Life Force of a Tree

According to the Chinese traditions that gave rise to such practices as *feng shui* and acupuncture, an invisible life force called *qi,* or *ch'i,* courses through everything in the universe. Trees, in particular, are regarded as wellsprings of the vital energy, drawing it out of the earth with their roots and setting it free through their leaves. In the human body, qi is thought to follow a circular path: It starts in the lower abdominal region, passes under the tailbone and up the spine to the head, before returning to the abdomen. A free flow of qi is considered essential to spiritual, mental, and physical well-being.

Another Chinese belief was that any living thing could respond to the qi in any other. Acting on this assumption, practitioners of the meditative art called *ch'i kung* developed an exercise for harnessing a tree's upward flow of qi to encourage the circulation of energy within the body. Before beginning such an exercise, the meditator takes pains to find a suitable tree for inspiration. Evergreens are considered the best, because they are not affected by seasonal changes. Maples, on the other hand, are generally avoided; tradition has deemed them unfriendly. Whatever the tree's variety, it should be neither too large nor too small, so that the reservoir of available energy is neither overpowering nor overly meager. The trunk should be straight and smooth, and—perhaps most important—the meditator must have a special feeling for the tree.

Once a suitable tree has been found, the meditator assumes a position, either sitting or standing, with his or her back up against the tree trunk. Then begins a process of concentration on pulling the qi up the spine to the head, while trying to detect an upsurge of power in the tree. A typical session lasts just ten minutes, and when it is complete, the ch'i kung practitioner takes care to guide the qi back to the abdomen. Excess qi in other parts of the body is believed to be potentially harmful. Rubbing the belly is the usual technique for easing the qi back home.

for instance, and the sunflower is one of several plants that track the sun in its course across the sky. Certain acacia plants display even more complex behavior, "paying" ants by giving them extra nectar, while the ants in turn fight off other, more predatory insects that might harm the plant. And in many areas, the common scrub weed responds to the hoofbeats of approaching cattle by sinking into a false wilt to make itself appear unappetizing.

At the beginning of the twentieth century, Austrian biologist Raoul Francé argued that these and other patterns of behavior implied that plants could move—much as humans do—of their own volition. Francé contended that most plants moved at such a slow pace that people didn't notice unless they paid very close attention. He himself, he said, had observed buds and twigs tracing exploratory circles in the air and tendrils reaching out to sense the plants' surroundings. After years spent scrutinizing such botanical activities, Francé concluded that plants were fully conscious, intelligent beings operating in a dimension of existence beyond human ken.

Although Francé's observations were dismissed by his contemporaries, his ideas gained new currency during the 1960s, when a series of novel experiments seemed to suggest that lie detectors could be used to measure the emotional responses of plants as well as those of human beings. This line of research was initiated late one night in 1966, when Cleve Backster, a security consultant, out of curiosity decided to measure how quickly the electrical potential of his secretary's potted dracaena—a small, broadleaved plant similar to a palm—would change when he gave it water.

Backster, a former CIA employee, was an expert in measuring the electrical potential of human skin with polygraph machines—lie detectors. Ordinarily, the electrodes of such a machine are pasted to a human subject's fingertips. A device called a galvanometer measures changes in the electrical conductivity of the skin, and a mechanical pen then traces these values on a moving strip of paper. If the subject experiences great stress—such as that involved in

lying—the relatively smooth line drawn by the pen rises jaggedly in an uncontrollable surge.

Backster reasoned that the same device could also be employed to measure changes in the conductivity of his secretary's dracaena. Pasting the electrodes to one of the plant's leaves just as he would to a human being's finger, he found that the resting measurement of the plant remained fairly steady, a response that would be expected from a calm human subject. So far, his results were unremarkable, because plants had been known since the 1870s to generate electrical signals. But when he supplied the plant with water, the next readings came as a surprise. According to his knowledge of physics, Backster expected that the circulating water would cause a slow increase in the plant's conductivity. Instead, as he later told the story, Backster was astonished to see the polygraph pen tracing the same kind of falling line that, in a human being, would indicate pleasurable relaxation.

Fascinated by this unexpected response, Backster decided to try to induce stress in the plant by burning one of its leaves. Before he had so much as reached for a match, however, the plant's charted line swung up into an agitated series of spikes similar to those caused by physical fear in a human being. It seemed to Backster that unless the sudden change in the electrical signal was sheer coincidence, the plant must have read his mind and reacted to the threatening situation as any thinking being would.

During the next several months, Backster explored this odd phenomenon using a number of innovative experiments. For one test, six of Backster's students secretly drew lots to determine which of them would rip apart one houseplant in front of another houseplant. The chosen student did the deed, and afterward, the surviving plant was exposed to each of the six students in turn. It had no reaction to five of them but greeted the sixth student with a barrage of agitated botanical signaling that correctly identified him as the killer.

Backster also tried some long-distance tests. Once, for

example, he wanted to measure the changes that might occur in a plant's electrical potential as its owner took a lengthy trip by airplane. After the trip, Backster determined that the measurement of the plant's energy potential increased each time the traveler tensed during landing.

In what would become his most famous experiment, Backster also tested the reactions of three philodendrons to the death—by boiling—of brine shrimp. As the shrimp died, Backster's polygraphs recorded electrical signals from his plants showing every sign of stress. But when his automated system poured in an equivalent amount of sterile water instead of shrimp, the plants remained passive and their signals steady.

By this time, Backster was committed to the idea of plant intelligence. When his plants failed to perform for a distinguished visitor, he declared they had "fainted" because the visitor had previously burned plants in her own laboratory. (In the same spirit, later experimenters sometimes blamed a lack of results on "sluggish" or "morose" plants.) On other occasions, Backster had to scramble to find plausible explanations for unanticipated changes in a plant's readings. Once he decided a suddenly active plant had been reacting to the death of bacteria in a sink where hot water was running; in another case he thought a plant had sensed the death of body cells when he painted iodine on a cut finger.

In 1968, Backster published some of his results in *The International Journal of Parapsychology* under the title "Evidence of Primary Perception in Plant Life." And as the news of his work became more publicized, others intrigued by the paranormal, including a respected IBM research chemist, undertook similar plant experiments, sometimes achieving the same results. In 1973, the publication of *The Secret Life of Plants,* a book by Peter Tompkins and Christopher Bird that discussed Backster's work and other paranormal plant research, produced an explosion of public interest. The notion quickly spread that, as the *New York Times* phrased it, plants "fear, love, hate, worry about dogs—who knows—may possess the power to read people's minds."

Reports of plant-human interactions began to surface in cities across the continent. In Los Angeles, the Reverend Franklin Loehr announced that plants that were prayed over grew faster than their neglected peers. A florist in Newark, New Jersey, declared that he sang to his flowers for an hour every day to improve their color and appearance. And singer-composer Dory Previn explained to the *Chicago Sun-Times* that at one time her plants had failed to grow because of Previn's own confused thinking. "Now that my head is straightened out a little more, my plants are doing better," Previn told the interviewer. "They're like friends. If you approve of them they approve of you. If you ignore them, they ignore you."

The Backster effect also gained a sympathetic ear in some military laboratories. In 1973, navy operations analyst Eldon Byrd reported he had duplicated some of Backster's experiments at the Naval Ordnance Laboratory in Silver Spring, Maryland. In his study, Byrd subjected plants to fire, dismemberment, even ultraviolet light, and then recorded their reactions. Like Backster, Byrd found that plants seemed to respond to the experimenter's intent as well as to his actions. At Fort Belvoir, Virginia, army researchers considered investigating the use of plants themselves as lie detectors in experiments that tried to measure human emotional response through the reactions of nearby plants.

Other scientists, however, were not so enthusiastic, as several carefully controlled attempts to replicate Backster's experiments failed to produce confirming results. In 1978, John Kmetz, a research associate at the privately funded Science Unlimited Research Foundation, became the latest in a series of scientists who worked closely with Backster to repeat his classic brine-shrimp experiment. Following Backster's advice,

Cleve Backster demonstrates a polygraph technique for measuring reactions of plants. The chart allegedly shows one plant's distress at the idea of being burned. In the 1970s, Backster persuaded New Jersey police to let him assist in a murder investigation. He hoped that plants might recognize the killer and register fear. The plants failed to respond, but it turned out that none of the suspects paraded before them was charged with the crime.

which included a rule that no other plants could be left in the room because they might tell new plants about previous experiments, Kmetz nevertheless failed to find any evidence of plant emotion. His research, wrote Kmetz, who went on to become the assistant dean of natural sciences at a New Jersey college, "led me to believe that his [Backster's] results . . . may represent only random electrical functioning of his electrode system. . . . I am suggesting that he is calling electronic noise a response." The noise theory might explain why other researchers of the day managed to

produce Backster-like effects in such inanimate objects as damp cloths. Backster himself has reported apparent emotional responses from shredded leaves, chicken eggs, human blood, and yogurt.

An equally cool-headed interpretation of the whole question of the secret life of plants has been offered by Anthony Huxley, a gardening expert and nephew of the writer Aldous Huxley. Posing the question, "Do plants feel?" Huxley answered "yes" and "no." Plants, he said, have a rudimentary system of "chemical messengers" that

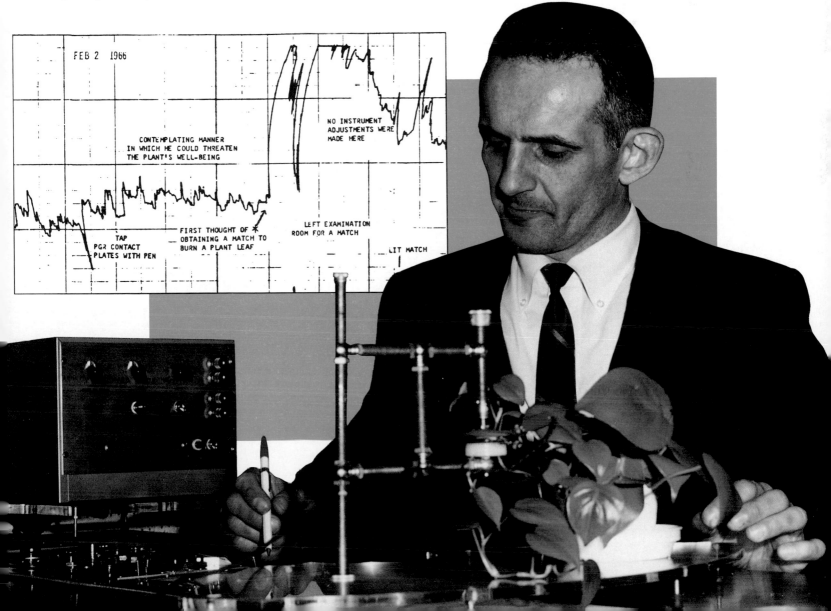

can trigger reactions to physical sensations, but those reactions do not signify emotional or intellectual perception.

According to Huxley, most so-called demonstrations of plant consciousness can be explained by a combination of plant physiology and human sentimentality. "One has finally to say that the imputation of fainting and telepathy in plants sounds like wishful anthropomorphism—that wish on man's part to make other organisms resemble him in as many ways as possible because, presumably, it makes them less alien and perhaps less frightening."

While Huxley and others were gently deflating claims of plant intelligence, yet another group of researchers was exploring the effects of a particular physical stimulus—musical sound—on plant development. Among the pioneers of the field that came to be called plant harmonics was T. C. Singh, head of the botanical department at India's Annamalai University. His work may well have been inspired by the ancient Indian tradition of *dohada,* a gardening technique that promotes growth by singing or playing to trees and plants.

According to one Western observer who visited Singh in 1950, the experimenter typically began work before sunrise, because the protoplasm inside a plant's leaves moves more slowly at night. In the predawn darkness, the visitor observed as Singh studied leaves through a microscope. Singh was watching protoplasm slowly streaming through the semitransparent leaf of a *Hydrilla* plant. Once the botanist switched on a motorized tuning fork, the protoplasm's motion accelerated dramati-

According to experiments conducted in the late 1960s by a college student named Dorothy Retallack—pictured here with her professor Francis Broman—plants not only respond to music but have their individual likes and dislikes. One of the plants below, for instance, supposedly revealed its distaste for avant-garde concert music by leaning away from the tape machine; the other was reportedly dying from too much exposure to so-called acid rock. Retallack found that music could have an effect on plant growth as well, as evidenced by the photograph at right, in which the roots of a rock-stimulated plant (far right) are sparse and distorted compared with those of a healthy control plant (near right).

cally, suggesting an increased metabolic rate that could lead in turn to faster growth.

In another experiment, Singh found that the sound of a violin had similar effects on some mimosa plants. After exposing the mimosas to violin music for a two-week peri-

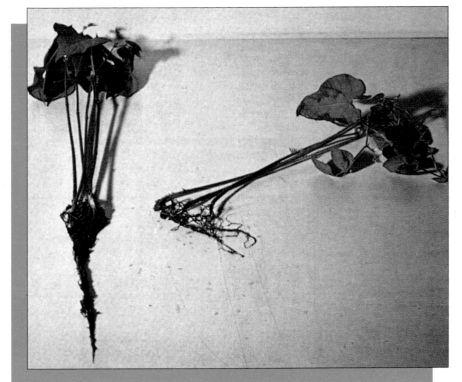

searchers at the University of North Carolina at Greensboro found that blasting turnips with "pink noise," which is similar to the sound of a jet engine, made the plants sprout more quickly than normal.

Meanwhile, as word of Singh's musical research spread, a skeptical Illinois botanist by the name of George E. Smith decided he would do some experimenting of his own. Smith planted identical crops of corn and soybeans in twin greenhouses, which were carefully regulated to produce the same artificial environments. One greenhouse he left alone. The other he outfitted with a phonograph that played George Gershwin's "Rhapsody in Blue" around the clock. Much to Smith's surprise, the crops in the music-filled room sprouted earlier and grew larger than those in the quiet greenhouse.

od, he discovered that the plants had two-thirds more *stomata*—the epidermal pores through which a plant "breathes"—than did similar specimens raised in relative silence. Even the cells of the serenaded plants seemed bigger and heartier. Based on this and other research, Singh later announced in an Indian agricultural journal that "beyond any shadow of doubt . . . harmonic sound waves affect the growth, flowering, fruiting, and seed-yields of plants." In food-poor India, the next natural step for Singh was to apply his findings to increasing crop yields. So he broadcast Indian ragas, or hymns, through loudspeakers directed toward a group of rice paddies; according to his records, the harvest from those paddies exceeded the yield from silent acreage by 25 to 67 percent.

Studies of what came to be called sound irradiation followed at other institutions, although inconclusive results eventually led to a falloff of academic research. Among the more promising findings were those of a team at the department of biology at the University of Ottawa, who reported in the mid-1960s that wheat seeds exposed to a single high-pitched tone later grew into adult plants more than twice as heavy as ordinary specimens. In another study, re-

The matter of musical influences on plant growth was taken to extremes by Dorothy Retallack of Denver, Colorado, a mother of eight who became the first grandmother to graduate from Temple Buell College. Intrigued by a magazine article about Smith's Gershwin experiment, Retallack persuaded her biology professor to let her do a study of the effects of sound on plants. For eight hours a day, in special fifty-six-foot-long environmental chambers that allowed close control of humidity, temperature, and light, Retallack's geraniums, philodendrons, corn, and radishes were exposed to a recording of a piano's F key played over and over. According to her report, the plants all died within two weeks' time. In a second chamber, however, similar plants were subjected to the same droning note for only three hours a day and did much better than a control group of plants housed in a third chamber with no sound.

Wondering whether the F note might have bored her hapless specimens to death, Retallack—herself a mezzo soprano and organist—decided to find out how plants would react to different kinds of music. She discovered, she said, that the plants seemed to share her own musical tastes—a revelation that struck some of her fellow students as somewhat suspicious.

Percussive rock music, which Retallack disliked, was revealed by her experiments to be extremely destructive, forcing plants to lean away from the loudspeakers and even killing one group of marigolds. Bach choral preludes and classical Indian ragas, on the other hand, were said to encourage marigolds and other plants to grow and thrive, causing them to bend toward the loudspeakers as if to increase their exposure to the airy strains. The plants also showed a marked, though less extreme, preference for jazz recordings by Louis Armstrong and Duke Ellington, but for some reason they displayed no reaction to country-and-western songs, a fact that puzzled Retallack. "Were the plants in complete harmony with this kind of earthy music?" she commented at the time. "Or didn't they care one way or the other?"

On October 16, 1970, Retallack had the opportunity to share her results with viewers across the nation in a report on the CBS Evening News, when she was asked by CBS co-ordinators to set up a rock versus raga experiment that would be filmed with time-lapse photography. Retallack later admitted she was "almost sick with nervousness" that the plants would not come through. Rising to the occasion, however, her botanical protégés duly leaned toward the mellifluous melodies of Ravi Shankar's sitar and away from the blasting strains of rock-and-roll.

Like Cleve Backster, Dorothy Retallack garnered her share of critics in the mainstream academic community, which in general tended to focus on her evident musical bias and her relative lack of scientific experience. Although he marshaled no specific arguments against Retallack's work, Frank Salisbury of the plant science department at Logan's Utah State University spoke for many conventional botanists when he told the *New York Times,* "I hate to just out-and-out say it's all baloney, but there's been an awful lot of pseudo-science in this field for years. Most of this stuff just doesn't have the right

kind of experimentation. Until that comes along I don't believe any of it."

Whatever the verdict may be with regard to plant awareness, though, the human need for greenery does unquestionably persist, even in the most technological of modern settings. During the 1980s and 1990s, humanity's age-old affinity for plants was vividly illustrated by the behavior and comments of Soviet cosmonauts living aboard the *Salyut-6, Salyut-7,* and *Mir* space stations, the first orbiting vessels to be manned for periods of several months without a break.

Plans for the stations had always included designs for special greenhouses equipped for zero gravity, but the purpose of the plants grown in these greenhouses was—at least originally—entirely utilitarian. All of the plants, including a small crop of orchids, were intended to help recirculate oxygen through the station (although a chemical process actually kept the atmosphere livable). Fresh foods and seasonings such as parsley, dill, onion, garlic, and wheat would also be grown, to supplement the cosmonaut diet. In addition, a small tray of cotton bolls would be included, to test the feasibility of space-grown textile material for longer journeys in the future. What the Soviets discovered, however, was that these pragmatic goals were of only secondary importance. All of the plants grown on board. they found, played a far more critical role in preserving the cosmonauts' mental health.

After a stretch of 185 days in orbit, one *Salyut-6* crew member who referred to plants as "our green friends" said he could not emphasize strongly enough the importance of the plant garden to his psychological well-being during his time on the space station. Another cosmonaut who spent 211 days on *Salyut-7* had the same reaction. "I think that in future flights there will be a lot of plants. They are simply essential to man in space," he said. "Back on Earth I had never loved tinkering in a garden. But onboard the space station it was as if I woke up all of a sudden. . . . A tiny leaf opened up and it seemed to fling open a bright window out into the world."

The Art of Feng Shui

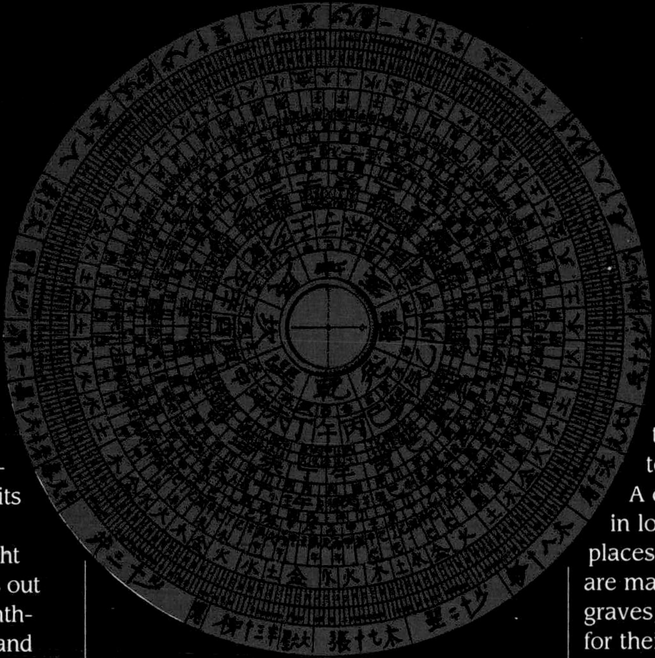

"There is a touch of magic light . . . amid confusion, peace; amid peace, a festive air. Upon coming into its presence, one's eyes are opened; if one sits or lies, one's heart is joyful. Here chi gathers, and the essence collects. Light shines in the middle, and magic goes out on all sides." Thus did one seventeenth-century Chinese describe a pleasant and auspicious place, where a fine balance of earth energies was achieved through careful attention to *feng shui*.

Feng shui is the Chinese name for the ambiance of a place and the art of harmonizing human works to their natural surroundings. Pronounced "fung-shway," the name means "wind-water" and implies the study of things that flow. The flow of *ch'i*, or *qi*—life energy, the earth's cosmic breath—is the essence of the art.

The feng shui master scrutinizes the earth as an astrologer does the heavens, seeking details that might affect future events. The goal is not to divine but to take a hand in positioning structures and influencing the flow of qi to invite the best possible outcome.

A common application of feng shui is in locating auspicious family burial places. The belief is that if the ancestors are made happy in their yin dwellings, or graves, they will secure great blessings for their descendants. But beneficial placement is also crucial for the yang dwellings of the living. The feng shui of a home or place of business is believed to bring good or bad luck in all aspects of life—including health, marriage, career, and reputation. If the feng shui of a schoolhouse is not favorable, for example, children will not learn quickly.

With so much at stake, and with the precepts of feng shui both complex and subjective, there is room for dishonest as well as honest practitioners. But the Chinese who can afford it consult a feng shui master when planning any kind of building or when starting a business.

Many feng shui consultants make use of the Lo Pan, or "heaven pool," compass (above), using its concentric rings to determine the astrological influences on a building site. Other adepts rely on the shapes and mystical traits of the four sacred animals below, as explained on the following pages.

BLACK TORTOISE

WHITE TIGER

GREEN DRAGON

RED PHOENIX

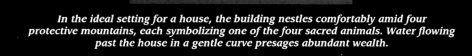

The yang dwellings of the living include not only homes but temples, banks, schools, factories, meeting halls, and other buildings. In the past, the Chinese designed all of these structures in accordance with feng shui principles. Even today in some parts of China and in other countries where Chinese have settled, there are consultants ready to advise householders on every stage of finding, building, or improving a home.

The first consideration is the land on which construction is planned or where a structure already exists. The site should welcome the flow of qi, with no obstructions blocking the front. Perfectly level land is not considered favorable, because it is thought to have no qi whatsoever. But the slopes that do exist should be gentle and flowing—never so steep as to

In the ideal setting for a house, the building nestles comfortably amid four protective mountains, each symbolizing one of the four sacred animals. Water flowing past the house in a gentle curve presages abundant wealth.

impede the flow of qi or to let prosperity roll away from a structure.

Nonetheless, mountains are believed to have rich endowments of qi and are in their own way highly desirable. Indeed, the ideal location for a house is a flat piece of ground halfway up the south side of a mountain *(above)*. Optimally, there will be additional hills to the east, west, and south—the last of these being low enough to permit an unobstructed view and an inward flow of qi and prosperity. In such an auspicious landscape, the sheltering mountain to the north is called the Black Tortoise. That to the east is the Green Dragon and should be a little larger than the White Tiger—the mountain to the west. The southern mountain is called the Red Phoenix.

These mountain creatures carry a multitude of mystical associations. Among other things, they are the four most important constellations of traditional Chinese astronomy, one in each quarter of the night sky. In the ideal homesite, the Red Phoenix is associated with fire, the Green Dragon with wood, the White Tiger with metal, and the Black Tortoise with water. The house itself, standing at the center, represents earth, the fifth great element of Chinese tradition, valued for its permanence and stability.

It is observed in the old feng shui texts that wind disperses qi, while water retains it, and over the centuries water has

come to symbolize wealth and opportunity. Nowadays, not only waterways but roads—with their streaming traffic—are said to be conduits for qi and to symbolize the flow of wealth. Desirable building sites are blessed with water in a pool or a gentle stream. Just as a current that flows

A crescent-shaped pool turned toward the house is said to bode well for career development.

too rapidly washes away valuable soil, so it also is deemed to flush away luck, prosperity, and money.

A road can have a similarly draining effect if it is situated too close to a house, and special care must be taken with the walkway or driveway that links a house to an avenue. The path should be wider than the main entrance of the home *(right)*, to allow the passage of a sufficient supply of qi. And in situations where excessive qi rushes in from the road, a

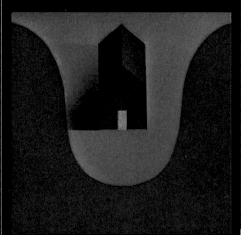

Set in the embracing curve of a river, this house should enjoy much prosperity, because water symbolizes money.

recommended to effectively increase the distance from the house to the thoroughfare *(middle right)*. It is also helpful if the house is buffered from the influences of a road by being set back in the middle third of its lot *(bottom right)*.

Straight lines aimed at a building are thought to produce a malevolent energy called *sha*. A dwelling should not lie in the path of a straight stretch of river or highway, for example. Nor should the spines of nearby roofs be pointing in its direction. These unlucky features are called secret arrows and direct sha toward the house and its occupants.

In fact, it is considered advisable that the entire surroundings of a domicile be evaluated with regard to their potential effect on the residents. Depending on their shapes, even distant mountains can influence human fortunes. A hill shaped like a dog may be regarded as a guardian, watching over the house. But an outcrop of rock with the contours of a rat may devour resources and deny prosperity.

The shape of a lot also carries portents. Square or rectangular lots are the most prized, because these shapes symbolize the element earth and thus confer solidity. The front of a lot is thought to be analo-

A path that widens as it leads away from the house is a hopeful sign for a promising career

gous to the present; the back represents the future. A plot of land that is wider in front than in back suggests good fortune for the present owners but dwindling prospects for their descendants.

In the real world, of course, perfectly shaped lots and mountainside sites are

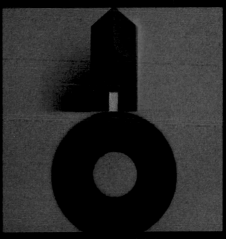

A circular driveway will allegedly bring a flow of qi and burgeoning opportunities for the residents.

extremely rare, and in urban settings not even half the lots can face the auspicious south. It is the task of the feng shui consultant, therefore, to identify problems and suggest possible remedies.

The usual approach is to regard each building site as a little world unto itself. The front of the lot and the front of the house are treated as if they were facing south, regardless of their compass orientation. And for properties lacking the ideal cluster of mountains, the feng shui master suggests ways to compensate for the presence of the missing sacred animals. An authoritative text called the *Yang-chai Ching,* or *The Classic of Dwellings,* prescribes the following substitutions: "All residences are honourable which have on the left flowing water, representing the Green Dragon; on the right a long path, symbolising the White Tiger; in the front a pool, for the Red Bird, and at the back a hill, the emblem of the Black Tortoise."

With such options available, almost any house can be given a favorable feng shui.

These remedies have the added benefit of enclosing the site on three sides, leaving the front open. Thus, the energizing qi will flow to the place and then be contained, to circulate and do the residents some good rather than simply dispersing. Feng shui experts advise that boulders, large trees, mounds, or walls in front of a house are likely to hinder the arrival of qi and can lead to bad luck. But these features have potential benefits in some circumstances. If a house cannot be built in the optimal middle third of a lot but must be set toward the front, then a tree, lamppost, or heavy stone placed at the rear of the lot balances the effect.

Indeed, all of the recommended feng shui remedies are designed to reconnect, balance, or stimulate the flow of qi. Traditional fixtures installed out of doors include lamps and mirrors to produce or reflect light; wind chimes to raise qi through the energy of sound; and objects that move, such as fountains, windmills, and mobiles. Judiciously placed trees, stones, paths, walls, and sheds can also have a useful effect in deflecting the sha of a secret arrow, for example, or in slowing a too rapid flow of qi.

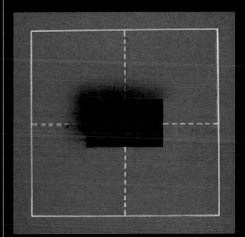

When a house is centered in its plot of land, the lives of its residents should remain pleasingly balanced

Within the house, as on the surrounding land, the feng shui practitioner's aim is to help qi circulate, letting it move freely but in a balanced and moderate way. The pictures on these pages illustrate, first, three features of interior design that help to achieve this aim, and then three that are less than ideal *(opposite)* but that have

The shape of a house should be balanced like this one to help its occupants to achieve balanced lives.

been corrected with remedies prescribed by feng shui experts. The remedies are used indoors for the same purpose as they are outdoors: to balance, encourage, or retard the flow of qi.

To help promote qi flow, the overall shape of a house should be regular and rectangular. Shapes based on the square are considered the most fortuitous, because four-sided figures harmonize with the four quarters of heaven and because right angles are thought to allow a good circulation of qi. Moreover, a balanced design in a domicile *(above)* is believed to promote balance in the lives of the people who occupy it.

Feng shui experts also look upon a house as a body with doors for mouths and windows for eyes. The hallways inside act as veins and arteries, conducting

qi among the rooms, whereas such features as interior doorways, corners, and beams are thought to have the potential to either enhance or impede the circulation. In keeping with this view, the feng shui patterns and problems of a house are seen as portents of corresponding bodily ills for the residents. Thus, a broken window may presage problems with vision.

Applying the principle that like imitates like, the feng shui expert studies the overall plan of a house for the influence it might have on the occupants' lives and interests. The most prominent rooms, especially those nearest the main entrance, will dominate the thoughts and activities of the people in the house. If a game room is near the front door, for example, it will encourage the residents to fritter away time and money on amusements. A kitchen, on the other hand, may lead to excessive eating or some other form of greed. In a house where a bathroom is large and central, the residents may spend disproportionate amounts of time coping with bladder problems or endlessly bathing and grooming themselves. A study that is too prominent promotes reclusive bookishness, but an inviting foyer or living room *(right)* draws in residents and visitors alike and promotes relaxed sociability.

From the feng shui perspective, a

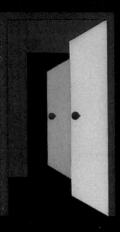

Doors should open inward to offer qi the easiest path. Two doors in succession should be exactly aligned and both hinged on the same side.

front door that leads into no room at all, but opens directly onto a wall, is most unfavorable, because it offers nothing but a dead end to anyone entering the house. Such an entrance inhibits qi and will inflict upon the residents a life of struggle and failure.

The room just inside the front door provides the first impression of a home. A good choice for that location is a sitting room, which conveys an invitation to relax.

The usual remedy is to hang a mirror on the obstructing wall, so that qi will be redirected to the interior.

The kitchen deserves a special place in a home, preferably on the south side. A kitchen's element is fire, and the food prepared there represents the wealth of the household. If the room is small or narrow, a mirror can be hung over the stove to symbolically increase the family's wealth by giving the appearance of doubling the number of burners. To safeguard whatever wealth does exist, the kitchen stove should never be too near a bathroom lest water coursing out of the house carry away the prosperity.

Each room in a house has its own best purpose, which a feng shui expert ascertains by evaluating the room's physical

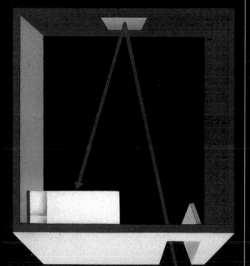

A bed is best in the corner opposite the door; failing that, a mirror can help to redirect the qi.

qualities, its compass orientation, and the implications of a mystical eight-sided figure called a *ba-gua (top right).*

Feng shui recognizes eight primary compass directions: the cardinal points of north, south, east, and west, plus the four "corner" points between them—north-east, southeast, southwest, and north-

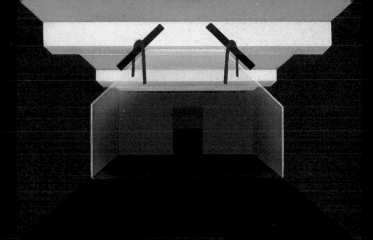

west. Each direction is assigned to one side of the ba-gua and attributed with unique properties, corresponding to the eight fundamental life concerns: health, wealth, fame, marriage, children, helpful acquaintances, career, and knowledge. When the ba-gua is superimposed on a house or on a room, one of these concerns becomes paramount in considering each part of the house or the room.

To counteract a beam's tendency to dampen energy, two bamboo flutes tied with red ribbons are hung at angles to form two sides of the auspicious ba-gua octagon.

The room marked for knowledge should be devoted to studious pursuits; a space on the children side of the octagon would be suited for a playroom. If there is a feng shui defect, an expert can judge by the orientation of the ba-gua what type of trouble the occupant is likely to encounter. Or, someone hoping for improvement in a particular area of life can attempt a feng shui remedy by reassigning rooms to different uses as indicated by the ba-gua. And there are other possible solutions: Wind chimes in the family area may defuse squabbling among relatives; or a fishtank or a talisman of the ba-gua itself may be placed in the wealth position to bolster family finances.

A projecting corner is always considered unfavorable, for it is believed to produce the malevolent sha. Whether the offending corner is part of a pillar or the bend in an L-shaped room, its threatening angles should be neutralized with mirrors, climbing vines, crystal balls, or wind chimes. Likewise, overhead beams are said to bear down on the flow of qi and be an oppressive influence. Experts advise altering such beams with bamboo

flutes *(above)* or a length of red fringe. A beam over a sleeper's head may cause headaches, or it may interfere with anticipated travels if it is above the feet. A bed should be moved from under a beam or at least turned so its length runs parallel to a beam rather than across it.

Because qi rushes wastefully fast through a line of doorways, a crystal ball is hung to impede the flow.

CHAPTER 4

Toward a New World-View

British biochemist and inventor James Lovelock's groundbreaking book *Gaia: A New Look at Life* presents the following scenario: A dedicated scientist, much distressed by the plight of starving children, resolves to find a way to increase the world's food production. Through genetic manipulation he succeeds in developing an improved strain of bacterium with an enormous capacity for gathering phosphate, an important nutrient for plant growth, from even the poorest of soils. He then adapts the new bacterium to live with a variety of crops, especially rice, a key source of food in many of the world's poorer countries.

The scientist conducts his first trials of the bacterium in England on wheat and several other cereal crops. The results of the experiment are extremely impressive; yields of all the crops increased substantially. To test the bacterium on rice, the scientist travels to Australia, never anticipating the mayhem that will soon follow.

Instead of forming a beneficial union with the rice, as it did with the cereal crops, the bacterium joins forces with a tough, tropical blue-green alga growing on the water surface of the paddy field. Together they create a new organism, a kind of superalga that grows unusually quickly, doubling in numbers every twenty minutes. Before long the entire paddy is covered with the organism.

Despite the valiant efforts of the scientist and his Australian colleagues to contain the new alga, it continues to spread, from the paddy to a stream and then on to sea. Within six months, more than 50 percent of the earth's oceans and the majority of its land surfaces are covered with blue-green slime. Like a cancer, the algae gradually displace all other living matter. As plants and animals die and decay, sulfur is released into the air, where it is oxidized to sulfuric acid and falls back on the earth in the form of acid rain, causing more death and decay. Eventually, the earth becomes as barren as Mars or Venus. Even the algae, with no other nutrients to feed upon, are unable to survive.

Lovelock's doomsday scenario is fiction, of course. And it is not likely to occur. As Lovelock points out, many scientists believe that nature has written too many roadblocks into the process of genetic coding for any newly created organism to run roughshod over the earth, destroying everything in its path. James Lovelock also believes that there are natural regulatory processes at work in the environment that would safeguard against such a catastrophe.

Yet his scenario does offer an important lesson: All living species on our planet are interconnected; when one species is tampered with, or destroyed, all are potentially threatened. "No longer can we merely regret the passing of one of the great whales, or the blue butterfly, nor even the smallpox virus," asserts Lovelock. "When we eliminate one of these from the earth, we may have destroyed a part of ourselves."

Today, more and more people are recognizing the interconnectedness of life on earth. They are beginning to see themselves as their ancient ancestors did: as one small part of a greater living whole. Their goal is not to conquer or control the earth but to live in harmony with nature and its hidden forces. Caring for the soil, whether it be by using special organic gardening methods or by communicating with invisible plant "spirits" or by healing the land with acupuncture, is considered particularly important, because it is from the soil that every living creature gathers sustenance and energy.

Several new scientific theories have contributed to this holistic and sometimes mystical view of earth. One of the most important of these theories is the brainchild of James Lovelock. Its origins can be traced back to the

early 1960s, when Lovelock was invited to the Jet Propulsion Laboratory near Pasadena, California, to help the National Aeronautics and Space Administration (NASA) determine whether or not life could exist on Mars. At that time, scientists believed that there was a good chance of discovering life on the Red Planet, although what form the life would take, nobody knew.

Lovelock decided that the best way to detect life on Mars, or on any other planet, was to study its atmosphere. He believed that any life that existed on Mars would almost certainly depend upon the atmosphere to help sustain itself. The life form would need to draw raw materials out of the atmosphere and to deposit some of the by-products of its metabolism into it. This meant that the chemical composition of the planet's atmosphere would be in a persistent state of disequilibrium.

Studying data from observations performed with a high-powered infrared telescope, Lovelock and his colleagues looked for signs of chemical disequilibrium in the atmosphere of Mars. They found just the opposite: an extremely dull and stable atmosphere that was dominated by carbon dioxide. Such evidence strongly suggested that the planet was lifeless—a conclusion later space explorations appeared to confirm.

Thinking about the possibility of life on Mars got Lovelock thinking more deeply about life on our own planet. When he returned to his home in Wiltshire, England, two questions kept nagging him. How can the earth's atmosphere, which consists of highly reactive gases, stay so constant? And how could such an unstable atmosphere be so perfectly suited for life? "It was then," Lovelock later wrote, "that I began to wonder if it could be that the air is not just an environment for life but is also a part of life itself."

From this seed of an idea, Lovelock has nurtured an exciting new scientific theory that has begun to transform not only how scientists see our planet but also how they view our relationship with it. According to Lovelock, the earth is an immense living organism that is both self-regulating and self-sustaining. All living matter on the planet, from bacteria to blue whales, from algae to ancient redwood trees, works together to maintain the earth's physical environment—its air, oceans, and soil—in a comfortable, life-giving state, in much the same way that all the organs and tissues of the human body interact with one another to keep the body alive. Furthermore, the evolution of earth's living species is so closely interwoven with the evolution of its physical and chemical environment that together they constitute a single evolutionary process. In other words, life itself is directly responsible for the development of the beautiful and bountiful planet earth; it is not simply a by-product of it.

Friend and neighbor novelist William Golding suggested that Lovelock christen the vast earth organism Gaia after the Greek earth goddess. Then, isolating himself in his country home, Lovelock began putting his theory down on paper. In 1979, he published his first book on the subject, *Gaia: A New Look at Life on Earth*. The work caused an immediate stir in the scientific community.

The Gaia hypothesis flies in the face of mainstream science, which looks at earth as a sphere of inanimate rock on which life appears as a chance occurrence. In the past, scientists have attributed the fact that the earth's atmosphere is hospitable for life to the planet's precise position in the solar system: If earth had had an orbit that was any closer to or farther from the sun, they said, life would not have evolved. Therefore, argue conventional scientists, human beings (as well as all other living organisms) should consider themselves fortunate that the earth is such an ideal home for life.

According to the Gaia concept, however, life has not only adapted to earth but has also adapted the planet to suit its own needs. Take the surface temperature of the earth, for example. Just as the human body regulates its own temperature, always holding it close to 98.6 degrees Fahrenheit, so does Gaia regulate her own average surface temperature, always keeping it around 55.4 degrees Fahrenheit. This temperature has stayed constant during the past 3,800 million years or so—about the same length of time that life has been present on the planet—even though the sun has become 25 percent brighter and hotter. What has kept earth from overheating? Life, says Lovelock. As the sun's rays have become stronger, earth's living organisms have drawn more and more carbon dioxide from the atmosphere, which has reduced the gas's greenhouse effect that would otherwise warm the planet's surface. Thus, to keep her temperature constant—and herself alive—Gaia has devised her own built-in cooling system as a means of offsetting the increasing heat from the sun.

Lovelock cites other evidence of life's ability to manipulate earth's physical environment into a stable, or homeostatic, state. The salinity of seawater, for example, has changed very little over the millennia, staying at a relatively constant 3.4 percent, despite the fact that salt is continually being washed off the land and into the sea by rain and rivers. Oxygen concentration in the atmosphere has kept stable at a steady 21 percent. If it were to go even slightly higher—to, say, 25 percent rather than the normal 21 percent—the earth's vegetation and all living things would spontaneously erupt in flames.

Such homeostatic behaviors are not merely coincidental, argues Lovelock. They are Gaia at work, regulating her planetary "body," adjusting her chemical and biological processes to keep herself alive and healthy. And she has successfully stayed alive for several billion years—far too long to be explained by luck alone. "For this to have hap-

Maverick British biochemist James Lovelock (below) relaxes in a sunny London park in 1989. Best known for his view of the earth as a living planet, Lovelock also invented the device that first detected damage-causing chlorofluorocarbons in the earth's atmosphere.

pened by chance," James Lovelock insists, "is as unlikely as to survive unscathed a drive blindfolded through rush-hour traffic."

Without life, Lovelock stresses, earth would be a very different planet. Its surface temperature would be around 554 degrees Fahrenheit, much too hot for life as we know it. Furthermore, the oceans would have dried up eons ago. The earth we are familiar with today, with its blue sky and its lush, green forests, would be a hot, dusty planet with a hazy, brownish red atmosphere, quite similar to its lifeless neighbor, Venus.

The concept of something as massive and as apparently inanimate as the earth being alive is difficult for many people to grasp; yet peoples of earlier eras who viewed the earth as a divine being would have had no problem with it. To help make Gaia more understandable, Lovelock and other Gaia enthusiasts compare the earth to a giant redwood tree. Although a 1,000-ton redwood tree is very much alive, more than 97 percent of its enormous trunk is dead wood. The living portion of the trunk—the part that carries water and minerals from the tree's roots to its leaves—consists of nothing more than a thin layer of tissue located under the bark. When the cells of this tissue die, they become part of the tree's outer bark or of its inner core of heartwood.

"Now in this way," says Lovelock, "a tree is very like the earth itself. Around the circumference on the surface of the earth is a thin skin of living tissue of which both the trees and we humans are a part. All of the rocks beneath our feet and the air above us is of course dead. But the air and the rocks are either the direct products of life or have been greatly modified by its presence."

When trying to conceptualize Gaia, it helps to step out of human time and into planetary time. Gaia moves on a much grander time scale than do humans. "For humans," says Lovelock, "a hundred thousand years is almost indistinguishable from infinity; to Gaia, who is about 3.6 eons old, it is equivalent to no more than three of our months." The passing of day into night and then back into day again is but a brief flick of the eye to Gaia. Only in expansive Gaian time can we see that earth moves and changes its appearance like any other living system. Its atmosphere and ocean currents swirl around the planet. Its land masses part, creating ever-changing coastlines, and then collide, pushing up huge mountain ranges. Its icy polar caps expand and

A Planet's Built-in Climate Control

To explain his Gaia hypothesis that life on earth regulates the terrestrial climate, James Lovelock often uses the hypothetical example of a planet much simpler than our world. As its name suggests, the imaginary Daisyworld harbors only one form of life—daisies, which may be dark, white, or gray. Simulated mathematically on a computer, the Daisyworld case shows how a single species could control the temperature of an entire planet.

The daisies in Lovelock's scenario require a moderate climate. None germinate at temperatures below 41° Fahrenheit and none survive above 104°. But the flowers face a potentially lethal threat: Daisyworld's sun, like our own, gets hotter as it ages. According to the computer, however, the flowers have a natural tendency to keep their environment within livable bounds. When the sun is young and cool, dark heat-absorbing daisies cover Daisyworld like a blanket *(left)*. As the sun gets hotter, conditions favor white daisies, which cool the planet by reflecting excess heat back into space *(right)*.

Lovelock has developed several other Daisyworld scenarios, some with rabbits that eat the daisies and coyotes that eat the rabbits. No matter how he tinkers with the program, he says, the system rectifies itself, maintaining a climate hospitable to Daisyworld life.

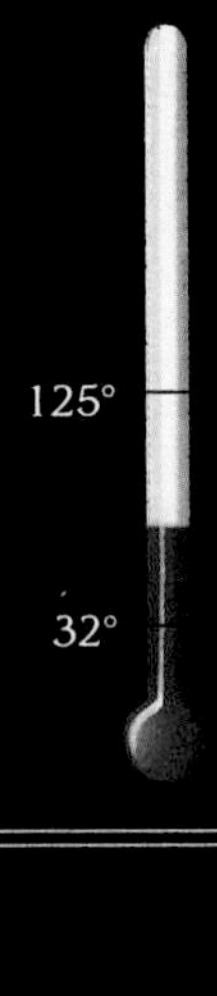

125°

32°

As a young sun sheds gentle light and heat on James Lovelock's fictitious Daisyworld (far left), dark daisies dominate the planet by virtue of their superior ability to capture warmth from the sun's rays. By storing solar energy, their dark petals are capable of raising the temperature of Daisyworld (see thermometer at left) to a level that is comfortable for all daisy life.

125°

32°

Ages later, warmer beams reach Daisyworld (above) from the maturing sun. Because the capacity to retain heat is no longer an asset, dark daisies become less common. Gray daisies, and even a few white ones, begin to spread. By reflecting part of the solar radiation (arrows), the lighter flowers help to keep Daisyworld's temperature at the same level it was before.

125°

32°

As Daisyworld's aging sun grows hotter still, white daisies—able to reflect a maximum of light and heat—take over the planet (above). For now, the white flowers preserve Daisyworld's equilibrium. One day, however, the sun's radiation will become too intense for even the purest white daisies to deflect, and Daisyworld will become a barren rock instead of a living planet.

contract from time to time, leaving behind rocky scars. Earth's character and demeanor are forever moving, forever changing.

Gaia has been a remarkable survivor. She has been able to recover from some extremely sharp blows. During the course of Gaia's life, at least thirty large meteors have crashed into earth, causing catastrophic damage. These monster meteors, approximately twice the size of Mount Everest and traveling at sixty times the speed of sound, strike earth on an average of about every 100 million years. Lovelock compares the damage done to Gaia by some of these collisions to a human burn affecting 60 percent of the skin. Some scientists believe that one such impact that occurred 65 million years ago caused the extinction of more than 60 percent of the plants and animals then living, including dinosaurs.

Yet Gaia has survived, even thrived, healing her physical wounds and creating new species to replace the old. Lovelock believes this ability to endure is yet more evidence of a powerful homeostatic system on earth, a system that is able to regain its life-sustaining balance even when severely jarred or damaged. For this reason, Lovelock believes that although humans may wound Gaia by dumping toxic wastes into her air and water and by destroying her forests and other natural resources, they cannot kill her. Gaia will adapt and survive, he argues, just as she has survived the gradual warming of the sun and the bombardment of immense celestial cannonballs.

Of course, not all environmentalists agree with Lovelock's assessment. Some see humans as a kind of planetary cancer, spreading rapidly and uncontrollably across the earth's surface. Astronaut Edgar Mitchell made such an observation while he was standing on the moon during the *Apollo 14* flight in 1971. Looking at earth as it hung suspended in space before him, Mitchell felt overwhelmed with the power and beauty of the planet and with his own sense of connectedness to it. Nevertheless, he also immediately recognized the vulnerability of the planet. "Beneath that blue and white atmosphere was a growing chaos that the inhabitants of planet earth were breeding among themselves," he later wrote. "[Human] population and technology were growing rapidly out of control."

Although Lovelock believes Gaia will most likely survive any illness created by humans, he acknowledges that with the cure may come human extinction. "As the ancient Greeks and other early civilizations realized full well, our own well-being depends first and foremost on how we treat the earth," warns Lovelock. "Gaia would reward mankind with her bounty when treated well, but equally she would revenge abuse." Thus a thoughtful modern man of science utters words eerily reminiscent of an ancient priest exhorting worshipers to pay proper homage to the earth goddess lest she punish their irreverence.

In fact, the twentieth century has heard a number of voices with messages similar to Lovelock's. Other thinkers have reflected on the possibility that this planet has powers we do not yet understand but that may be vastly important to the future of humanity. Many other people, sometimes acting out of a kind of blind faith instead of a carefully thought-out theory or philosophy, have taken personal, practical steps to treat the earth with the reverence due a divine being—and have apparently been rewarded with her abundant largesse.

At about the same time that Lovelock was developing his unorthodox theory of Gaia, another maverick English scientist, Rupert Sheldrake, was formulating an even more controversial notion about earth and a special kind of unseen hidden force. According to Sheldrake's provocative yet bizarre hypothesis, the form and nature of all things on earth, from the shape of a particular crystal to the ability of birds to migrate, depend on mysterious forces, which the biochemist calls morphic fields (from the Greek *morphe*, meaning "form").

Each type of organic system, whether it be beech trees, flu viruses, or human beings, has its own special field. Through a process of "morphic resonance" the individual members of a system can tune in to the behavior and expe-

The Strange Case of the Hundredth Monkey

One day in 1953 on the island of Koshima, a macaque monkey named Imo picked up a sand-covered sweet potato supplied by researchers studying her species. Carefully, she rinsed it in a stream. Then she ate the potato.

In the years that followed, that simple meal led to a controversial theory, put forward in 1979 by zoologist Lyall Watson. According to Watson, Imo's potato washing was unprecedented for a macaque, and the practice at first spread slowly. But in 1958, he claimed, something astonishing happened. Suddenly almost every monkey on Koshima was washing potatoes. "Not only that," he wrote, "but the habit seems to have jumped natural barriers and to have appeared spontaneously . . . in colonies on other islands and on the mainland."

Conceding that the available facts were sparse, Watson supplemented his account with some imagined details. "Let us say," he wrote, "that the number [of potato-washing monkeys] was ninety-nine and that at eleven o'clock on a Tuesday morning, one further convert was added to the fold. . . . The addition of the hundredth monkey apparently carried the number across some sort of threshold, pushing it through a kind of critical mass." Once the number of potato washing macaques reached critical mass, he said, knowledge of the skill spilled over as if by telepathy to other monkeys on Koshima and elsewhere.

A similar effect in humans, wrote Watson, could explain the way that ideas "spread through our culture."

For other observers, this phenomenon seemed to confirm Rupert Sheldrake's idea that members of a species learn from one another through morphic fields, mysterious energies said by Sheldrake to pervade the earth.

For all the fascinating implications of the hundredth-monkey effect, however, many of the events on which Watson based the idea apparently never occurred. In 1985, Ronald Amundson, a professor of philosophy at the University of Hawaii, showed that Watson had misinterpreted the original Japanese studies of the Koshima macaques.

Amundson found that the reports confirmed that Imo had invented potato washing and taught it to other monkeys. But the articles showed that only two macaques learned the skill in 1958, ruling out Watson's story of a burst of learning. The reports also stated that monkeys sometimes swam between islands—providing a plausible transmission route for the habit.

Watson later told reporters that he did not dispute Amundson's findings. The hundredth-monkey idea, he explained, was a rhetorical device. "It is a metaphor of my own making, based . . . on very slim evidence and a great deal of hearsay. I have never pretended otherwise."

Unaware of scientific scrutiny, a red-faced Japanese macaque washes a sweet potato in a convenient stream. The monkeys have also been observed separating wheat from sand by throwing mixed handfuls into the sea and gathering the floating grain after the sand sinks.

rience of other members of that system, like television sets picking up distant transmissions. Each member can then use the information contained in its system's morphic field to modify its own behavior.

According to Rupert Sheldrake's theory, once an animal learns a new skill, others of the same species should subsequently become capable of acquiring that ability more easily, even if they have had no contact with the animal that originally mastered the skill. For example, after the first dog learned how to catch a Frisbee back in the 1970s, it should have been easier for all dogs, anywhere in the world, to become adept at leaping in the air and catching the spinning toy.

Indeed, past experiments with rats seem to confirm that such learning does occur. During the 1920s, a Harvard University psychologist, William McDougall, noticed in a series of experiments that successive generations of rats learned to escape from a unique type of water maze with increasing skill. Because each generation of rats was bred from par-

ents who had already mastered the maze, McDougall assumed that the rats simply passed the skill on to their offspring genetically.

To rule out the possibility that he had not just selected quicker-learning rats as parents, McDougall repeated his experiment, this time breeding new rats only from the slowest-learning ones in each generation. If genetic selection were at work, each successive generation of rats should have exhibited a decreasing ability to maneuver through the maze. To McDougall's astonishment, he found just the opposite to be true: Successive generations of rats learned at an even faster rate.

Later, two separate groups of researchers—one in Scotland, the other in Australia—repeated McDougall's experiments using an identical type of water maze. Not only were McDougall's findings confirmed, but these later researchers reported that the first generation of their rats learned even more quickly than McDougall's initial generations had done. In fact, the

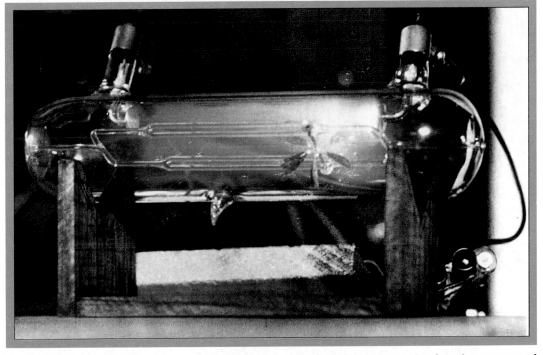

Scottish researchers found that some of the first rats they tested immediately ran through the maze without making a single error. To Sheldrake, these findings strongly indicated that genes and heredity cannot explain all learning behaviors.

Sheldrake first conceived of his theory of morphic fields while he was working as director of biochemistry and cell biology at England's Cambridge University. In 1974, needing more time to develop the intricacies of his theory, he left Cambridge for India, where he took a less demanding job studying the physiology of tropical crops. Four years later, feeling that he was ready to put his ideas on paper, Sheldrake quit his job and moved to a Christian ashram. While in this self-imposed seclusion, he finally pulled together his ideas about morphic fields, publishing *A New Science of Life: The Hypothesis of Formative Causation* in 1981.

The book was immediately denounced by much of the scientific community. The magazine *Nature,* one of the world's most influential scientific journals, published a scathing editorial review of the book under the heading ''A Book for Burning?'' ''This infuriating tract,'' proclaimed the editorial, ''. . . is the best candidate for burning there has been for many years.'' Condemning Sheldrake's theory as ''an exercise in pseudoscience,'' *Nature's* editors suggested that *A New Science of Life* be banished to its only proper place on the bookshelf—''among the literature of intellectual aberrations.''

Not all members of the scientific community were so damning, however. Indeed, many were intrigued by the scientific questions Sheldrake's theory raised and encouraged their peers to give it a fair hearing rather than dismissing it outright. One scientist wrote that Sheldrake's hypothesis was ''an astonishing challenge to orthodox theories of plant and animal development.'' Another rebuked *Nature's* editors for attacking Sheldrake's ideas, saying the critics had shown ''contempt for a whole, lively tradition of puzzlement and creative thought.''

The editors at another respected British journal, the *New Scientist,* were also less harsh with Sheldrake. They noted that his morphic-field hypothesis met the necessary criterion for a scientific theory: It could be proved either right or wrong. Rupert Sheldrake himself encouraged other scientists to test his hypothesis in the laboratory, emphasizing that if experiments proved him wrong, he would abandon his notion.

Soon after the publication of *A New Science of Life,* an independent think tank called the Tarrytown Group in Tarrytown, New York, offered a $10,000 prize to the person who performed the best test of Sheldrake's hypothesis. Ac-

cording to the rules of the contest, it did not matter whether the winning experiment confirmed or refuted Rupert Sheldrake's hypothesis, as long as the experiment was well designed and executed.

Two cowinners were announced in the summer of 1986, and both of their experiments seemed to give some credence to the existence of morphic fields. As it happened, both of the studies involved human beings dealing with unfamiliar languages.

One of the experiments was conducted by Gary Schwartz, professor of psychology and psychiatry at Yale University. He asked groups of students who did not know Hebrew to guess the meanings of a set of three-letter Hebrew words; half of the "words" were not words at all, just scrambled Hebrew letters. The students also rated their level of confidence for each guess. Schwartz's results showed that the students were significantly more confident when they were guessing the meaning of the real words, especially the most commonly used words. Schwartz believes that the results show an "intuitive awareness" of Hebrew among the students.

Language was also the focus of the cowinning experiment, which was conducted by Alan Pickering of Hatfield Polytechnic in Hatfield, England. He instructed one group of students to look at Persian words and another group to look at nonsense words that were made to look Persian; he then asked both groups to attempt to recall the words that they had seen. None of the students had any prior knowledge of the Persian language. Nevertheless, the students who saw the real words exhibited better recall.

Although he was delighted with these results, Sheldrake believes that much more evidence is needed to prove that morphic fields exist. Indeed, as critics point out, the explanation for the results of the language experiments may not have anything to do with morphic fields but may instead reflect an unconscious deciphering of the patterns that exist in real language.

Basic to Sheldrake's theory of morphic fields is a belief that not all of earth's powerful forces and energies are yet understood or even acknowledged. This idea is also the guiding principle behind biodynamic farming, one of the more fascinating and ecologically rooted agricultural movements of the twentieth century. A mixture of mysticism and science, with a little witchlike potion mixing thrown in, biodynamic farming holds that the blanket of soil that covers the earth is a living organism that contains its own life forces. Biodynamic farmers believe that in order for soil to produce a healthy crop year after year, its life forces must be continually replenished. The duty of the farmer, therefore, is to care for the soil correctly, using specially prepared organic composts and sprays. According to biodynamic theory, food that is grown in such soil will be not only richer in nutrients and better tasting but more spiritually balanced as well, which makes it as nourishing for the human soul as it is for the body.

Biodynamic farming was the creation of Rudolf Steiner, an Austrian social philosopher and scientist who had, by the 1920s, recognized the inherent dangers that

Following the biodynamic methods of Austrian psychic Rudolf Steiner, the Virginia farmer at left stuffs manure into a dried cow horn. Below, two Steiner enthusiasts prepare to bury 850 similarly doctored horns. When unearthed several months later, the horns will contain a dry, odorless substance. Biodynamic farmers believe one cup of this material, mixed with twelve gallons of rainwater, can rejuvenate four acres of soil.

chemical farming presented to the earth. In 1924, just a year before his death at age sixty-four, Steiner delivered a series of eight lectures to a group of German and Austrian farmers who were concerned not only about the poor fertility of their overworked soil but also about a dismaying increase

man who is generally credited with being the founder of the organic farming movement, had also taken to the lectern to preach the perils of chemical farming and the salvation of the soil through organic methods. Howard's message, however, was clearly down-to-earth; the composting and or-

ganic farming practices that he advocated were simple and straightforward, the kind that had been practiced by farmers for centuries. Rudolf Steiner's methods, on the other hand, were quite esoteric, involving elaborate rites and rituals.

As a self-professed clairvoyant and former member of the mystically oriented Theosophical Society, Steiner believed that for organic matter to work its magic on soil it must first be vitalized and spiritualized by special cosmic forces. For this purpose he developed nine special biodynamic soil solutions, which he referred to simply

in plant and animal diseases. In these lectures, which were later compiled into a small book called simply *Agriculture,* Steiner outlined his strong belief in a need to protect the earth from the destructive forces of modern farming methods. He told the farmers that they should turn away from artificial fertilizers and should feed their soil a diet of rich organic compost and humus. Their soil was dying, he informed them, and it was up to them to save it.

Steiner was not the first person to advocate a return to chemical-free, or organic, farming. Several years earlier, Sir Albert Howard, a British officer and botanist and the

as preparations 500 to 508. Each preparation, he stressed, has a slightly different practical purpose—number 500, for example, promotes root growth, whereas number 508 helps prevent plant rust and other fungal diseases. Yet each one also has the grander purpose of returning "beneficial energies" to the land.

Perhaps surprisingly, considering the practicality of farmers in general, Steiner's 1924 lectures were a success. The farmers who attended immediately formed an "experimental circle" to discuss and work out ways to put his ideas into practice. Other farmers, first in Europe and then in

North America and other parts of the world, soon followed suit, eager to replenish the energy of their own spiritless soil. Most heard about biodynamics through the efforts of the Anthroposophical Society, an international organization Steiner had established in 1913 to practice what he called Spiritual Science. Steiner believed traditional science was too material, focusing only on the physical realm and ignoring how nature is affected by otherworldly influences. After the 1924 lectures, biodynamics quickly became an important part of the society's activities.

Steiner's organization still has a headquarters in Dornach, Switzerland, and his prescripts for protecting the soil continue to be followed by thousands of farmers and backyard gardeners around the world, from the North American plains to the Australian outback. This unique form of organic agriculture is especially popular in Europe, where many stores sell only biodynamically grown food. In the Netherlands, biodynamic farming has become so well accepted that the government hires experts in biodynamics to pass their knowledge on to other farmers. The United States and Canada also have a good share of biodynamic farmers; their produce, which is usually more expensive than conventional organically grown food, can be found at many health-food stores and food co-ops.

Biodynamic farming requires great dedication and attention to detail. To properly inoculate the earth with the right cosmic forces, Steiner said, the prescribed solutions must be painstakingly prepared with ingredients that sound more like a witch's brew—things such as yarrow blossoms stuffed into the bladder of a buck deer and oak bark ground up and placed in the skull of a cow—than standard fertilizers.

Some of the preparations must be buried for several months before they are considered to be ready for use. In one of his 1924 lectures, Rudolf Steiner explained with characteristic spiritual obtuseness why preparation 500, which is essentially cow manure packed into a cow's horn, needs to be buried: "By burying the horn with its filling of manure, we preserve in the horn the forces it was accustomed to exert within the cow itself, namely the property of raying back whatever is life-giving and obtained from the astral plane." The manure, Steiner added, is capable of gathering life forces not only from the horn but also from the soil in which it is buried. "And so, through the winter, in the season when the earth is most alive, the entire content of the horn becomes inwardly alive," he explained. "All that is living is stored up in this manure."

The decayed manure is removed from the cow's horn in early spring, before the planting season begins. Small amounts are then stirred into buckets of collected rainwater warmed to human body temperature. The mixing process, which lasts an hour, is very ritualistic: The solution must be stirred for twenty seconds one way, then twenty seconds the other, in order to bring the cosmic life forces of earth and the universe into harmony. When the mixing is done, the solution is ready to be sprayed onto a field. As in homeopathic medicine, only very small amounts are actually used: About one-fourth cup of manure added to three gallons of water is considered enough to energize an entire acre of farmland.

In addition to making and using Steiner's esoteric and earthy preparations, biodynamic farmers follow the practice of moon watching to determine when to plant and when to harvest their crops. For example, many biodynamic farmers

Developed by Steiner follower Maria Thun, these charts associate the moon's zodiacal position with earth, water, light, and warmth—elements crucial to plant growth. The table below shows that when the moon is in Taurus, Virgo, or Capricorn, earth is ascendant, and the time is right to plant root vegetables.

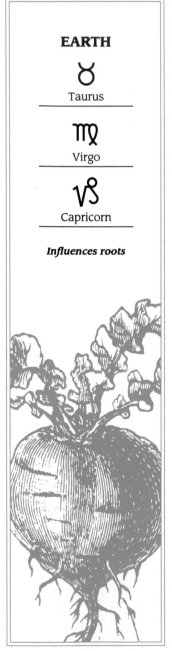

EARTH

☉
Taurus

♍
Virgo

♑
Capricorn

Influences roots

WATER

♓
Pisces

♋
Cancer

♏
Scorpio

**Influences leaves
and leafy plants**

plant new crops two days before the appearance of a full moon, in the hope of making the best use of its gravitational pull. Some also turn to the positioning of the planets for planting and pruning guidance. Steiner taught that each aspect of a plant—its root, leaf, flower, and fruit—is influenced by the movements of the planets across the zodiacal sky. Therefore, the biodynamic farmer must work with particular plants on those days when planetary positioning is most favorable for the part of the plant that he or she wants to encourage to grow. Lettuce and spinach would be tended on the "leaf" days, for instance, or turnips and potatoes on the "root" days.

To control insect pests, biodynamic farmers follow a more practical scheme, the age-old gardening custom of companion planting. This practice pairs plants that seem to encourage each other to grow, in some cases by one plant repelling insects that would attack the other. Garlic, for example, is planted among rose- and raspberry bushes in order to deter Japanese beetles; pot marigolds are planted among tomatoes and asparagus to repel tomato worms and asparagus beetles.

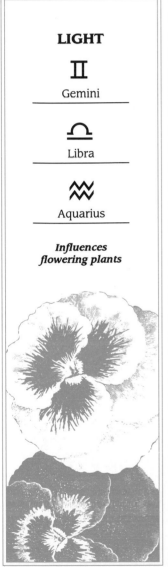

LIGHT

♊︎

Gemini

♎︎

Libra

♒︎

Aquarius

Influences flowering plants

Sometimes insect pests are collected and stewed in a pot of water; after the brew is strained and cooled, it is sprayed onto vegetables and fruit trees, where it is supposed to function as a kind of natural pesticide. Various plants, such as common horsetail, are also brewed into a tea and sprayed onto crops in an effort to help prevent plant diseases. For biodynamic gardeners, these out-of-the-ordinary pesticides offer yet another way of balancing the forces of nature. The followers of Rudolf Steiner stress, however, that the ultimate balancing must be done within the soil itself. According to biodynamic theory, healthy soil that has been well infused with the earth's life forces is the only guarantee of healthy, insect-resistant plants.

With its peculiar methods and spiritualistic overtones, biodynamic gardening leaves some farmers—including many who do embrace less chimerical organic methods—skeptical and wary. Steiner himself realized that his ideas would be difficult to accept. "I know perfectly well that all of this may seem utterly mad," he said during one of his lectures. "I only ask you to remember how many things have seemed utterly mad which have nonetheless been introduced a few years later."

Indeed, some scientists are now finding there may be merit to at least some of Steiner's "mad" ideas. Researchers in Central America, for example, have found that cotton crops have less of a problem with insect infestations when planted during certain phases of the moon. And studies conducted in Mexico seem to show that the technique of burning pests—in this case, beetles—to release substances that ward off other pests may also have some validity.

Although Steiner recognized that plants derive most of their life forces through nutrients in healthy soil, he also believed that they were continually drawing energy from the swirl of life that surrounds them above ground. Birds in particular, he stressed, have a powerful influence on the flowering and fruiting of plants. Through their song and the air vibrations caused by the flapping of their wings, Steiner asserted, the birds help to stimulate plant growth.

Some thirty-five years after Steiner's death, in the demilitarized zone between North and South Korea, a young army recruit from Minnesota named Dan Carlson witnessed a tragic scene that would eventually lead him to share Steiner's belief that birdsong helps plants grow. On that cold winter day in 1960, Carlson watched in horror as a young Korean mother purposely put her four-year-old son under the wheels of a moving two-ton truck, crushing his

WARMTH

♈︎

Aries

♌︎

Leo

♐︎

Sagittarius

Influences fruit, seed, and grain

legs. As a doctor was summoned, the woman tearfully explained that she had been compelled to cripple her son so that they could beg enough food to feed him and her other two children.

Profoundly moved by the incident, Carlson decided he would devote the rest of his life to finding a new and inexpensive way to grow food on even the poorest parcel of land. Upon returning to the United States, he enrolled in a horticulture and agriculture program at the University of Minnesota and began studying how plants grow. He quickly concluded that when a plant cannot get sufficient nourishment from the soil, it might still survive if it is able to take in sustenance through the tiny mouthlike

stomata on its leaves. These openings generally serve the purpose of exchanging moisture and gases with the air around a plant. But Carlson reasoned that an inexpensive liquid nutrient—in quantities so small it would be virtually lost if poured onto the ground—could conceivably nourish a plant sufficiently to enable it to grow even in the most arid of soils if sprayed directly onto the leaves. He was not certain, however, how it would be possible to get the stomata to take on this new feeding function.

Inspired by the studies of the American researchers who followed in the footsteps of T. C. Singh in examining the effects of sound on plants, Carlson began to search for frequencies that might spur stomata to open and take in nutrients. After a great deal of trial-and-error experimentation, he discovered what he felt was the right combination of frequencies and harmonics. He demonstrated the

The Water Goddess versus the Experts

It was a classic case of modernization versus tradition—with an unlikely final twist. Beginning in 1978, the government of Indonesia joined forces with the Asian Development Bank in a $24 million plan to modernize rice growing on the island of Bali. By modern farming methods, they hoped to increase crop yields and thus the supply of food for the nation.

Like most aspects of Balinese life, rice farming had been by tradition a highly spiritual pursuit. Throughout the terraced fields, prayer stations like the one here, as well as larger shrines, honored the rice spirits. Even irrigation was a matter of religious ritual. If a farmer wanted to water his fields, he consulted the keepers of the shrine directly upstream. They in turn spoke with the farmers and priests just up the hill, until the chain of requests rose to a temple beside one of the island's major water sources, a lake in an extinct volcano. According to Balinese belief, this lake was home to the water goddess Dewi Danu, whose high priest Jero Gde lived in the nearby temple

and managed the island's irrigation.

Then came modernization. Advisers encouraged farmers to plant three crops a year, instead of the two that Jero Gde had permitted. The result was little short of ecological disaster. Farmers discovered that keeping fields planted year-round enabled insects and rats to survive and multiply. Pesticides intended to eliminate the vermin also killed fish and eels that had lived in the paddies and provided protein for the local diet.

Then help came from an unexpected quarter. Learning of the problem during field research on Bali, researchers at the University of Southern California developed a computer program that calculated the long-term effects of both the traditional system and the modern approach. Taking into account not only crop schedules but also rice strains, likely rainfall, and the level of social cooperation, the program produced comparative maps of the island under each system that included graphs of crop yields. The maps easily proved that the fragile rice paddies were best managed in the age-old way. As a result, the Jakarta government curbed its modernization efforts in 1988. Farming on the island once again followed the guidance of Dewi Danu and her vindicated high priest.

sounds for a friend, Minneapolis music teacher Michael Holtz, and asked him to find music into which the frequencies could be merged.

Upon hearing the strange string of chirplike pitches that Carlson produced, Holtz immediately recognized that the sounds were very similar to the early morning concert of birdsongs outside his bedroom window. "It was thrilling to make that connection," Holtz later recalled. "I began to feel that God had created the birds for more than just freely flying about and warbling. Their very singing must somehow be intimately linked to the mysteries of seed germination and plant growth."

Today, Carlson's idea of spraying a plant's leaves with a liquid nutrient while at the same time bombarding it aurally with special birdlike sonic pitches is being tried experimentally on several farms around the world. One Florida orange grower who uses the method reports that his fruit is not only larger, juicier, and sweeter than before but also has 121 percent more vitamin C. A Pennsylvania dairyman notes that after his cows began eating hay made from sonically grown alfalfa, their milk production jumped from 6,800 to 7,300 pounds per hundredweight of cow—even though the cows were eating a quarter less feed. And a representative of a farmers' association in Pakistan says that his potato yields increased by 150 percent and his corn yields by 85 percent after he used Carlson's methods. Although these isolated experiments have not persuaded many other farmers to turn on the stereo in their fields, Carlson remains hopeful that his methods will soon be more widely adopted. "I would challenge anyone to look at the model gardens I've set up, examine the radiant health of the plants, witness the remarkable fructification, and taste of this fruit," he says. "It is all done with nothing but affection, natural nutrients, and sound."

The idea that the earth has unseen forces that can be tapped to help plants grow in even the sorriest of soils is a central belief of a remarkable experimental community that is located in a remote area of northern Scotland. For the past quarter of a century, this community, known as the Findhorn Foundation, because of its location near a village named Findhorn, has been a mecca for New Age disciples looking to find a more direct way of getting in touch with the hidden forces of nature.

Findhorn's story first became public in 1965. In the autumn of that year, a county horticultural adviser drove to a trailer park located on a sandy, wind-swept stretch of land overlooking the Firth of Moray. He was on his way to get a soil sample from a rather unlikely garden. The garden belonged to Peter Caddy, an ex-Royal Air Force squadron leader and former hotelkeeper who had moved to the trailer park three years earlier with his wife, Eileen, their three sons, and a spiritualist friend named Dorothy Maclean. Out of a gravelly patch of gorse and sand, Caddy had created a miracle garden of sorts, where he grew sixty-five types of vegetables, twenty-one kinds of fruits, and more than forty different herbs.

Although the Findhorn garden was thriving, Caddy, who had never sown a single vegetable seed before moving to the community, had asked the county adviser to test his soil, because he was concerned that it might be lacking in nutrients. After taking one look at Caddy's soil, the adviser said that it would undoubtedly require at least two ounces of sulfate of potash per square yard. When Caddy replied that he did not believe in using artificial fertilizers, that he preferred natural compost and wood ash instead, the adviser shook his head and reported that he considered such substitutes to be totally inadequate.

The adviser took a soil sample from Caddy's garden back to Aberdeen. Returning six weeks later with his analysis, the adviser admitted to Caddy that he was totally baffled. The analysis had found that there were no nutrient deficiencies in the soil; in fact, rare trace elements were present in the sample. Amazed that such rich soil could be created on such poor land, the adviser asked Peter Caddy to participate in a radio debate with a professional gardener who advocated conventional chemical means of gardening. Caddy consented.

During the radio show, Caddy credited his extraordinary gardening success to the use of compost and other organic gardening techniques, as well as plain hard work. This practical message was well received, and throughout the following year, a steady trickle of curious gardeners began to visit the Findhorn Foundation. Yet, like the county agricultural adviser who had traveled to Findhorn before them, many of these visitors, especially those who were experienced in organic growing methods, were bewildered by what they found. They felt that ordinary organic methods could not explain the radiant health of the flowers, fruits, and vegetables grown on that otherwise infertile stretch of land. "The vigor, health and bloom of the plants in the garden at midwinter on land which is almost a barren powdery sand cannot be explained by the moderate dressings of compost, nor indeed by the application of any known cultural methods of organic husbandry," noted an agricultural expert from the United Nations. "There are other factors and they are vital ones."

Peter Caddy also believed that there were other factors at work in his gardens, although he did not acknowledge this publicly until 1968. In that year he professed his belief that the world is a living sentient organism and that nature is empowered with many as yet unsuspected and quite powerful forces. Through the spiritual gifts of friend Dorothy Maclean, Caddy said, he had been able to communicate directly with invisible angel-like creatures that he called devas, from a Hindu word meaning "beings of light." The devas, Caddy explained, control the "nature spirits," broader forces of nature that permeate all of earth's differ-

ent physical forms, from clouds to cauliflower, from rain to red maples. Each species of plant, he emphasized, possesses its own deva.

Through Maclean, the devas of the plants in Caddy's garden gave him almost daily practical instructions about how to water, feed, mulch, and otherwise care for them. Maclean would consult the devas in the course of her daily meditations and then pass on the messages she received. One day, for example, the spinach deva sent her the following message: "If you want strong natural growth of the leaf, the plants will have to be wider apart than they are at the moment. By leaving them as they are, you will get overall as much bulk in the leaves, perhaps a little tender, but with not as strong a life force."

Maclean also received messages from a spirit, which she and Caddy called the Landscape Angel, that "overlighted" the entire garden. This being, a kind of spokesangel for all the devas, was usually more general in its advice than its colleagues were. It stressed the importance of humans radiating love and positive emotions while they work in a garden, particularly while preparing the soil. But it also gave practical advice, passing on to Caddy such information as how to make compost, when to water, and how to apply liquid manure.

Today, more than 100 people live and work at the Findhorn Foundation, and many more visit annually from every corner of the world to study how to communicate and collaborate with the forces of nature, whether it be through devas, through nature spirits, or simply through developing a more sensitive awareness of plants and other living beings. Yet the members of the community believe that Findhorn is much more than just an experiment in organic gardening. Wrote longtime resident David Spangler: "[We] are

A landscaped mandala of soil and plants, the Findhorn herb garden (far left) supplies seasonings, medicine, dye, cleansing agents, and fragrant herbs to its small community, whose ideal of closer spiritual union with the natural world is described in part on the blackboard at left. By communing with the plants they grow, residents of the Findhorn Foundation like the farmer above hope to achieve harmony with all life on earth.

Supposedly neutralizing negative earth energies on a Vermont farm in 1990, psychic farmer Sig Longren first locates subterranean lines of force with a freshly cut dowsing rod (below, left). After identifying the boundaries of a force line with a so-called aurameter (top right), Longren hammers a concrete reinforcing rod deep into the line's center (bottom right). According to Longren, the rod functions much like an acupuncturist's needle by altering the earth's natural flow of energy.

not just growing vegetables and flowers on barren sand. [We] are working with the processes of emergence and drawing out of earth its potential. This actualization of the living Self of the planet is what has transformed the barren sand into a garden.''

Far from Findhorn, on a communal farm in the red-earth Cotswold Hills of southern England, another group of nature visionaries turned to the ancient Eastern technique of acupuncture as a means of healing and revitalizing their tired land. After purchasing the farm, its owners discovered that the valley in which it lay was devoid of most wildlife and that people who came to visit for more than a few hours developed a stomach ailment, whether or not they drank the water. Eventually, the community reached the conclusion that the source of their trouble was a new quarry that had been carved out of the earth approximately fifty miles away. They believed it had created an imbalance of energy that had somehow focused on their valley. Only by shielding the valley from the quarry's ''bad'' energy, or *sha*, they reasoned, could their land's life forces become balanced once again.

The community's leader and another member were both experienced earth acupuncturists, people who have taken the Chinese medical practice of puncturing the human body with special needles to cure disease and have adapted it to heal the earthen ''body'' of Gaia. To rid their farmland of its bad energies, the two men began by pounding twenty wooden stakes, their tops wrapped with copper wire, into the ground at specially selected sites. Within days, the mysterious stomach ailments went away. More stakes were then added to fill in any possible ''holes'' through which negative energy could still flow from the quarry. Seemingly in response to this action, the wildlife began to return. Finally, in an effort to restructure the energy flow and return an atmosphere of peace to the land, the men hammered more than sixty additional stakes—iron ones this time—into the ground. Gradually, over a period of two years, the members of the community said that they noticed a feeling of deep peace and quiet had spread over the valley—like ''the deep silence of a cathedral,'' as one observer described it.

Perhaps the acupuncture restored health to the Cotswolds farm, or maybe it was simply the sound farming methods of the owners that caused the improvement. It is even possible that the perception of the soil's increased healthiness as well as the sense of peace were actually self-induced changes of attitude in which the stakes functioned as charms. In any case, the story is a good illustration of how individual human efforts apparently can have a positive impact on the health of the planet. Many scientists believe, however, that such individual efforts may not be enough to counter the enormous global effects of acid rain, massive deforestation, greenhouse gases, and other ecological assaults on the earth.

James Lovelock and others who share his view of a living earth strongly believe that Gaia will probably be able to survive any human threat to her health. Whether human beings can survive, however, is less certain. If we continue to change the global environment against the preferences of Gaia, Lovelock warns, we may encourage her to replace our species with one that is more compatible.

Like other environmentalists, Lovelock believes that living in harmony with the earth is a personal responsibility and that personal efforts can, on a large scale, have a lasting effect. ''It all depends on you and me,'' he says. ''If we see the world as a living organism of which we are a part— not the owner, nor the tenant, not even a passenger—we could have a long time ahead of us and our species might survive for its allotted span.''

Lovelock's sentiment echoes that of the American Indian chief Seattle of the Suquamish tribe, who told the U.S. government in 1854, during a dispute over his people's lands: ''If men spit upon the ground, they spit upon themselves. This we know, that the earth does not belong to man; man belongs to the earth. . . . Man did not weave the web of life, he is merely a strand in it. Whatever he does to the web, he does to himself.''

ACKNOWLEDGMENTS

The editors wish to thank the following individuals and institutions for their valuable assistance in the preparation of this volume:
A. Altan Akat, Director General, Museums and Artifacts of the Ministry of Culture, Ankara, Turkey; François Avril, Conservateur, Département des Manuscrits, Bibliothèque Nationale, Paris; Horus Buchhandlung, Bonn; The Earthquake Research Institute of the University of Tokyo, Tokyo; Reinhard Eisele, Augsburg, Germany; Sig Longren, Greensboro, Vermont; Lino Pellegrini, Milan; Dr. H. Preuschoft, Ruhr Universität, Bochum, Germany; Alexa Roberts, Historical Preservation Department, Navajo Nation, Window Rock, Arizona; Dr. Jim Swan, The Institute for the Study of Natural Systems, Mill Valley, California; O. Gurkan Toklu, Director, Anadolu Medeniyetleri Muzesi, Museum of Anatolian Civilizations, Ankara, Turkey; Stephen Trimble, Salt Lake City; Ann Washatko, House of Mystery, Hungry Horse, Montana.

BIBLIOGRAPHY

Adair, Gene, *George Washington Carver*. New York: Chelsea House, 1989.

Alexander, Marc, *British Folklore*. New York: Crescent Books, 1982.

Alldritt, Charles, *Tree Worship with Incidental Myths and Legends*. Auckland, Australia: Charles Alldritt, 1965.

Allen, Judy, and Jeanne Griffiths, *The Book of the Dragon*. London: Orbis, 1979.

Allen, Oliver E., and the Editors of Time-Life Books, *Atmosphere* (Planet Earth series). Alexandria, Va.: Time-Life Books, 1983.

Allen, Paula Gunn, "American Indian Mysticism." *Shaman's Drum*, mid-fall 1988.

Amundson, Ron:
"The Hundredth Monkey Phenomenon." *The Skeptical Inquirer*, summer 1985.
"Watson and the 'Hundredth Monkey Phenomenon'." *The Skeptical Inquirer*, spring 1987.

Asimov, Isaac, *Exploring the Earth and the Cosmos*. New York: Crown, 1982.

Baker, Margaret, *Folklore and Customs of Rural England*. Totowa, N.J.: Rowman and Littlefield, 1974.

Baldwin, Gordon C., *Indians of the Southwest*. New York: G. P. Putnam's Sons, 1970.

Bangs, Richard, and Christian Kallen, *Islands of Fire, Islands of Spice: Exploring the Wild Places of Indonesia*. San Francisco: Sierra Club Books, 1988.

Banyard, P. J., *Natural Wonders of the World*. Secaucus, N.J.: Chartwell Books, 1978.

Beck, Peggy V., and A. L. Walters, *The Sacred: Ways of Knowledge, Sources of Life*. Tsaile, Ariz.: Navajo Community College, 1977.

Becker, Robert O., and Gary Selden, *The Body Electric: Electromagnetism and the Foundation of Life*. New York: Morrow, 1985.

Bluth, B. J., and Martha Helppie, "Soviet Space Stations as Analogs." NASA Grant NAGW-659, NASA Headquarters, Washington, D.C., May 18, 1987.

Bord, Janet, and Colin Bord:
Ancient Mysteries of Britain. Manchester, N.H.: Salem House, 1986.
Sacred Waters: Holy Wells and Water Lore in Britain and Ireland. London: Granada, 1985.

Buchanan, Keith, Charles P. Fitzgerald, and Colin A. Ronan, *China*. New York: Crown, 1980.

Campbell, Joseph, *The Masks of God: Primitive Mythology*. New York: Viking Press, 1959.

Cattell, J. McKeen, and Dean R. Brimhall, eds., *American Men of Science: A Biographical Directory*. Garrison, N.Y.: Science Press, 1921.

Cavendish, Richard, ed., *Man, Myth & Magic*. New York: Marshall Cavendish, 1985.

Clayre, Alasdair, *The Heart of the Dragon*. Boston: Houghton Mifflin, 1986.

Collier, John, *On the Gleaming Way*. Denver: Sage Books, 1962.

Condit, Ira J., *Ficus: The Exotic Species*. Riverside, Calif.: University of California, 1969.

Cook, Roger, *The Tree of Life: Image for the Cosmos*. New York: Avon Books, 1974.

Corliss, William R., comp., *Unknown Earth: A Handbook of Geological Enigmas*. Glen Arm, Md.: Sourcebook Project, 1980.

Cotterell, Arthur, *The Macmillan Illustrated Encyclopedia of Myths & Legends*. New York: Macmillan, 1989.

Crockett, James Underwood, and the Editors of Time-Life Books, *Trees* (The Time-Life Encyclopedia of Gardening). New York: Time-Life Books, 1972.

Davidson, H. R. Ellis, *Scandinavian Mythology*. New York: Peter Bedrick Books, 1982.

Delgado, Pat, and Colin Andrews, *Circular Evidence*. London: Bloomsbury, 1989.

Dobzhansky, Theodosius, *Genetics of the Evolutionary Process*. New York: Columbia University Press, 1970.

Dogra, Bharat, *Forests and People*. New Delhi, India: Bharat Dogra, 1983.

Doolittle, Jerome, and the Editors of Time-Life Books, *Canyons and Mesas* (The American Wilderness series). New York: Time-Life Books, 1974.

Dupuis, Jean, *Marvellous World of Trees*. Transl. by David Macrae. London: Abbey Library, 1976.

The Editors of Time-Life Books:
Japan (Library of Nations series). Alexandria, Va.: Time-Life Books, 1985.
Mystic Places (Mysteries of the Unknown series). Alexandria, Va.: Time-Life Books, 1987.

Eitel, Ernest J., *Feng-Shui*. London: Synergistic Press, 1984.

Eliade, Mircea:
Myths, Dreams and Mysteries. Transl. by Philip Mairet. New York: Harper & Row, 1960.
Patterns in Comparative Religion. Cleveland: World, 1963.

Emboden, William A., *Bizarre Plants: Magical, Monstrous, Mythical*. New York: Macmillan, 1974.

The Encyclopedia of Organic Gardening. Emmaus, Pa.: Rodale Press, 1978.

Erdoes, Richard:
The Native Americans: Navajos. Ed. by Marvin L. Reiter. New York: Sterling, 1979.
The Rain Dance People. New York: Alfred A. Knopf, 1976.

Erdoes, Richard, and Alfonso Ortiz, eds., *American Indian Myths and Legends*. New York: Pantheon Books, 1984.

Evers, Larry, ed., *The South Corner of Time: Hopi, Navajo, Papago, Yaqui Tribal Literature*. Tucson, Ariz.: Sun Tracks, 1980.

Ewart, Neil, *The Lore of Flowers*. New York: Sterling, 1982.

Facts & Fallacies. Pleasantville, N.Y.: Reader's Digest Association, 1988.

Findhorn Community, *The Findhorn Garden*. New York: Harper & Row, 1975.

Facelière, Robert, *Greek Oracles*. Transl. by Douglas Garman. New York: W. W. Norton, 1965.

Frazer, James George:
The Golden Bough: A Study in Magic and Religion. New York: Macmillan, 1950.
The New Golden Bough. Ed. by Theodor H. Gaster. New York: New American Library, 1964.

Fuller, Paul, and Jenny Randles, *Controversy of the Circles: An Investigation of the Crop Circles Mystery* (report). British UFO Research Association, June 1989.

Furst, Peter T., "An Indian Journey to Life's Source." *Natural History*, April 1973.

Gartlein, Carl W., "Unlocking Secrets of the Northern Lights." *National Geographic*, November 1947.

Gettings, Fred, *Secret Symbolism in Occult Art*. New York: Harmony Books, 1987.

"The Ghost-Dance Religion, and the Sioux Outbreak of 1890," in the *Annual Report of the Bureau of American Ethnology*, XIV, 2, Washington, D.C.

Gimbutas, Marija, *The Language of the Goddess*. San Francisco: Harper & Row, 1989.

Gliedman, John, "Beyond the Brain's Boundaries." *Science Digest*, February 1983.

Goldsmith, Edward, and Nicholas Hildyard, eds., *The Earth Report: The Essential Guide to Global Ecological Issues*. Los Angeles: Price Stern Sloan, 1988.

Gordon, Lesley, *The Mystery and Magic of Trees and Flowers*. Exeter, England: Webb & Bower, 1985.

Graves, Tom, *Needles of Stone*. London: Turnstone Press, 1978.

Great Disasters. Pleasantville, N.Y.: Reader's Digest Association, 1989.

Hawken, Paul, *The Magic of Findhorn*. New York: Harper & Row, 1975.

Heffern, Richard, *The Complete Book of Ginseng*. Millbrae, Calif.: Celestial Arts, 1976.

Hemleben, Johannes, *Rudolf Steiner: A Documentary Biography*. Transl. by Leo Twyman. Sussex, England: Henry Goulden, 1975.

Hitching, Francis, *Earth Magic*. New York: William Morrow, 1977.

Hole, Christina, *Encyclopaedia of Superstitions*. New York: Hutchinson, 1961.

Huxley, Anthony, *Plant and Planet*. New York: Viking Press, 1974.

Itoh, Teiji, *Gardens of Japan*. New York: Kodansha International, 1984.

Jacob, Dorothy, *A Witch's Guide to Gardening*. New York: Taplinger, 1964.

James, Peter, "A Visit to Troytown." *The Unexplained* (London), Vol. 13, Issue 148.

Jones, Charles, ed., *Look to the Mountain Top*. San Jose, Calif.: Gousha, 1972.

Jordan-Smith, Paul, "The Serpent and the Eagle." *Parabola*, August 1989.

Keegan, Marcia, *The Taos Indians and Their Sacred Blue Lake*. New York: Julian Messner, 1972.

Kmetz, John M., "Plant Primary Perception: The Other Side of the Leaf." *The Skeptical Inquirer*, spring/summer 1978.

Kurtz, Paul, ed., *A Skeptic's Handbook of Parapsychology.* New York: Prometheus Books, 1985.

LaChapelle, Dolores, *Earth Wisdom.* Los Angeles: The Guild of Tutors Press, 1978.

Loh, Jules, *Lords of the Earth: A History of the Navajo Indians.* New York: Crowell-Collier, 1971.

Lovelock, James:
The Ages of GAIA. New York: W. W. Norton, 1988.
GAIA: A New Look at Life on Earth. Oxford, England: Oxford University Press, 1988.
"Lunar Grip on the Tides." *LIFE,* July 4, 1969.

McDonald, Kimla, "Living Earth: Protecting Sacred Places in the American Southwest." *Shaman's Drum,* winter 1986-1987.

McGuire, Edna, *The Maoris of New Zealand.* New York: Macmillan, 1968.

Mann, W. Edward, and Edward Hoffman, *The Man Who Dreamed of Tomorrow: A Conceptual Biography of Wilhelm Reich.* Los Angeles: J. P. Tarcher, 1980.

Marbach, William D., "A New Theory of Causation." *Newsweek,* July 7, 1986.

Meaden, George Terence, *The Circles Effect and Its Mysteries.* Wiltshire, England: Artetech, 1989.

Michell, John:
The Earth Spirit. New York: Thames and Hudson, 1975.
Megalithomania. Ithaca, N.Y.: Cornell University Press, 1982.
The New View over Atlantis. San Francisco: Harper & Row, 1983.
The Traveler's Key to Sacred England. New York: Alfred A. Knopf, 1988.

Miller, Hamish, and Paul Broadhurst, *The Sun and the Serpent.* Cornwall, England: Pendragon Press, 1989.

Momaday, N. Scott, "I Am Alive . . . ," in *The World of the American Indian.* Washington, D.C.: National Geographic Society, 1974.

Nature's World of Wonders. Washington, D.C.: National Geographic Society, 1983.

Nazario, Sonia L., "Are Organic Foods Spiritual Enough?" *The Wall Street Journal,* July 21, 1989.

Newton, Douglas, and Brian Brake, "The Maoris." *National Geographic,* October 1984.

Ortiz, Alfonso, "Farmers and Raiders of the Southwest," in *The World of the American Indian.* Washington, D.C.: National Geographic Society, 1974.

Page, Jake, and Susanne Page, *Hopi.* New York: Abrams, 1982.

Palmer, Eve, and Norah Pitman, *Trees of South Africa.* Amsterdam: A. A. Balkens, 1961.

Parker, Ronald B., *Inscrutable Earth.* New York: Charles Scribner's Sons, 1984.

Pennick, Nigel, *The Ancient Science of Geomancy: Man in Harmony with the Earth.* London: Thames and Hudson, 1979.

Pfeiffer, John E., *The Emergence of Man.* New York: Harper & Row, 1969.

Phallic Tree Worship. Varanasi, India: Bharat-Bharati, 1971.

Philpot, J. H., *The Sacred Tree or The Tree in Religion and Myth.* London: Macmillan, 1897.

Piggott, Juliet, *Japanese Mythology.* New York: Peter Bedrick Books, 1983.

Radice, Betty, *Who's Who in the Ancient World.* Baltimore: Penguin, 1973.

Rajaonah, Voahongy, "The Sacred Trees of Madagascar." *UNESCO Courier Magazine,* May 1990.

Reich, Wilhelm, *Ether, God and Devil.* Transl. by Therese Pol. New York: Farrar, Straus and Giroux, 1973.

Ricciuti, Edward R., *The Devil's Garden: Facts and Folklore of Perilous Plants.* New York: Walker, 1978.

Richardson, P. Mick, *Flowering Plants: The Encyclopedia of Psychoactive Drugs.* New York: Chelsea House, 1986.

Rossbach, Sarah:
Feng Shui. New York: E. P. Dutton, 1983.
Interior Design with Feng Shui. New York: E. P. Dutton, 1987.

Russell, Peter, *The Global Brain.* Los Angeles: J. P. Tarcher, 1983.

Scott, Donald, *The Psychology of Fire.* New York: Charles Scribner's Sons, 1974.

Sen Gupta, Sankar, *Sacred Trees across Cultures and Nations.* Calcutta, India: Indian Publications, 1980.

Service, Alastair, and Jean Bradbery, *A Guide to the Megaliths of Europe.* London: Granada, 1979.

Sharkey, John, *Celtic Mysteries: The Ancient Religion.* London: Thames and Hudson, 1979.

Sheldrake, Rupert:
A New Science of Life. Los Angeles: J. P. Tarcher, 1981.
The Presence of the Past. New York: Times Books, 1988.
"Rupert Sheldrake's Hidden Force." *Science Digest,* October 1981.

Shepherd, A. P., *A Scientist of the Invisible.* London: Hodder and Stoughton, 1971.

Simpson, Jacqueline, *European Mythology.* New York: Peter Bedrick Books, 1987.

Sjöö, Monica, and Barbara Mor, *The Great Cosmic Mother.* San Francisco: Harper & Row, 1987.

Spangler, David, *Emergence: The Rebirth of the Sacred.* New York: Dell, 1984.

Spencer, Baldwin, and F. J. Gillen, *The Arunta: A Study of a Stone Age People.* London: Macmillan, 1927.

Starr, Douglas, "Artificial Intelligence." *Omni,* September 1990.

Stirling, Matthew W., "Indian Tribes of Pueblo Land." *National Geographic,* November 1940.

Sutphen, Dick, *Sedona: Psychic Energy Vortexes.* Ed. by Dawn Abbey. Malibu, Calif.: Valley of the Sun, 1986.

Swan, Jim, "Sacred Places: Can Traditional Wisdom and Science Support Each Other?" *Shaman's Drum,* winter 1986-1987.

Temple, Robert K. G., *China: Land of Discovery.* Wellingborough, England: Patrick Stephens, 1986.

Thomas, Keith, *Man and the Natural World.* New York: Pantheon Books, 1983.

Thompson, William Irwin, ed., *GAIA: A Way of Knowing.* Barrington, Mass.: Lindisfarne Press, 1987.

Tompkins, Peter, and Christopher Bird:
The Secret Life of Plants. New York: Harper & Row, 1973.
Secrets of the Soil. New York: Harper & Row, 1989.

Vitaliano, Dorothy B., *Legends of the Earth.* Bloomington, Ind.: Indiana University Press, 1973.

Vittachi, Anuradha, *Earth Conference One.* Boston: Shambhala, 1989.

Walters, Derek:
Chinese Geomancy. Dorset, England: Element Books, 1989.
Feng Shui: The Chinese Art of Designing a Harmonious Environment. New York: Simon & Schuster, 1988.

Waltham, A. C., *The World of Caves.* New York: G. P. Putnam's Sons, 1976.

Waters, Frank, *Book of the Hopi.* New York: Viking Press, 1963.

Watson, Lyall, *Lifetide: The Biology of the Unconscious.* New York: Simon & Schuster, 1979.

Weiner, Jonathan, *Planet Earth.* Toronto: Bantam Books, 1986.

Williamson, Hugh Ross, *The Flowering Hawthorn.* New York: Hawthorn Books, 1962.

Winkless, Nels, III, and Iben Browning, *Climate and the Affairs of Men.* New York: Harper's Magazine Press, 1975.

Yang Jwing-Ming, *Chi Kung: Health & Martial Arts.* Jamaica Plain, Mass.: Yang's Martial Arts Association, 1987.

PICTURE CREDITS

The sources for the pictures are given below. Credits from left to right are set off by semicolons, from top to bottom by dashes.

Cover: Artwork by Bryan Leister. 6, 7: Frederick C. Taylor, Andover, Hants, England. 8, 9: From *Circular Evidence* by Pat Delgado and Colin Andrews, Bloomsbury, London, 1989. 10, 11: Frederick C. Taylor, Andover, Hants, England. 12, 13: From *Circular Evidence* by Pat Delgado and Colin Andrews, Bloomsbury, London, 1989. 14, 15: D. Hudson/ Sygma. 17: Will Williams, Stansbury, Ronsaville, Wood, Inc. 18: Yorkshire Television, Leeds, England. 20: The British Library, London—Frederick C. Taylor, Andover, Hants, England. 21: From *Fortean Times #53*; from *Circles from the Sky*, ed. by George Terence Meaden, Souvenir Press, London, 1991—from *Circular Evidence* by Pat Delgado and Colin Andrews, Bloomsbury, London, 1989. 22: Adam Woolfitt, Susan Griggs Agency, London. 23: Yanki, courtesy Museum of Anatolian Civilizations, Ankara, Turkey. 26: J. Zuckerman/Westlight. 26, 27: Nimatallah/Ricciarini, Milan. 28: Galen Rowell/Mountain Light, Albany, Calif. 30: Mick Sharp, Caernarvon, Gwynedd, Wales. 31-33: Homer Sykes, London. 34: R. Ian Lloyd, Singapore. 35: Leong Ka Tai, Hong Kong. 37: F. C. Tyler; Hereford and Worcester County Library, Hereford, England. 39: Jerry Jacka, Phoenix (detail from page 49). 40, 41: Kurt Kummels/Superstock. 42: Terry E. Eiler, *Mugwump.* 43: Jerry Jacka, Phoenix. 44, 45: David Meunch, Santa Barbara, Calif. 46, 47: Art Kane, Pasadena, Calif. 48, 49: Jerry Jacka, Phoenix. 51: Will Williams, Stansbury, Ronsaville, Wood, Inc. 53: Anthony Suau/Black Star. 55: Smithsonian Institution Photo No. 79-14705. 56, 57: Taikichi Irie, Nara Prefecture, Japan. 60, 61: Earthquake Research Institute of the University of Tokyo; Jim Mondenhall © National Geographic Society. 62: Humberto N. Serra, Rome, courtesy Biblioteca Angelica, Rome. 63: Paul Chesley/Photographers Aspen. 65: Tom Bean, Flagstaff, Ariz.; Dick Canby, Sedona, Ariz. 68, 69: Philip Griffiths/Magnum. 71: Superstock. 72, 73: George Silk for *Life.* 74: Allen Kennedy/Janet and Colin Bord, Wales. 75: Bates Littlehales © 1961 National Geographic Society. 78, 79: Judy Canty/Stock-Boston. 80, 81: Kevin Schafer/Peter Arnold Inc. 82: G. Ziesler/Peter Arnold Inc. 83: David Hiser/Photographers Aspen. 84, 85: Stephen J. Krasemann/Peter Arnold Inc. 86, 87: David Meunch, Santa Barbara, Calif. 89: Will Williams, Stansbury, Ronsaville, Wood, Inc. 90: From *The Arunta* by Baldwin Spencer and F. J.

Gillen, Macmillan, London, 1927. 91: Paul Broadhurst, Launceton, Cornwall, England. 92: R. Berriedale-Johnson/ Panos Pictures, London. 93: D. Laine-Hoa-Qui, Paris. 94: Richard Lannoy, from *The Tree of Life* by Roger Cook, Avon, New York, 1974. 95: Reinhard Eisele, Augsburg, Germany. 96: ET Archive, London. 97: British Library, London. 98: Zigy Kaluzny/Gamma Liaison UP July 17, 1989, pp. 116-117 filed 541-PL. 100: *Botanical Magazine* LXXIII 1847, T. 4296. 101: From *Bizarre Plants* by William A. Emboden, Macmillan, New York, 1974. 102: Michael Holford, Lough-ton, Essex, England. 103: Homer Sykes, London. 104: Tuskegee University Archives. 106: Yong's Martial Arts Association, Jamaica Plain, Mass.; from *The Illustrated Encyclopedia of Trees* by Herbert Edlin and Maurice Nimmo, Harmony Books, 1978. 109: Backster Research Foundation, San Diego. 110, 111: George Crouter, Denver. 113: From *Chinese Geomancy* by Derek Walters, Element Books, Dorset, England, 1989—Fred Holz, from *Empires Ascendant* (Time Frame series) by the Editors of Time-Life Books, Alexandria, Va., 1987. 114-117: Yvonne Gensurowsky. 119: Will Williams, Stansbury, Ronsaville, Wood, Inc. 121: Terry Smith for *People,* December 25, 1989. 122, 123: Matt McMullen. 125: Dr. H. Preuschoft, Bochum, Germany. 126: Syndication International, London. 127: From *Ether, God and Devil* by Wilhelm Reich, Farrar, Straus and Giroux, New York, 1973. 128, 129: Courtesy Harper & Row Publishers from *Secrets of the Soil* by Peter Tompkins and Christopher Bird. 132: R. Ian Lloyd, Singapore. 134, 135: From *The Findhorn Garden* by the Findhorn Community, Harper & Row, New York, 1975. 136: Chazz Sutphen.

INDEX

Numerals in italics indicate an illustration of the subject mentioned.

Time-Life Books Inc.
is a wholly owned subsidiary of
THE TIME INC. BOOK COMPANY

President and Chief Executive Officer: Kelso F. Sutton
President, Time Inc. Books Direct: Christopher T. Linen

TIME-LIFE BOOKS INC.

Managing Editor: Thomas H. Flaherty
Director of Editorial Resources: Elise D. Ritter-Clough
Director of Photography and Research: John Conrad Weiser
Editorial Board: Dale M. Brown, Roberta Conlan, Laura
Foreman, Lee Hassig, Jim Hicks, Blaine Marshall, Rita
Thievon Mullin, Henry Woodhead

PUBLISHER: Joseph J. Ward

Associate Publisher: Ann Mirabito
Editorial Director: Russell B. Adams
Marketing Director: Ann Everhart
Director of Design: Louis Klein
Production Manager: Wendy Foster
Supervisor of Quality Control: James King

Editorial Operations
Production: Celia Beattie
Library: Louise D. Forstall
Computer Composition: Deborah G. Tait (Manager),
Monika D. Thayer, Janet Barnes Syring, Lillian Daniels

Library of Congress Cataloging in Publication Data
Earth Energies by the editors of Time-Life Books.
    p. cm.—(Mysteries of the unknown.)
    Includes bibliographical references and index.
    ISBN 0-8094-6512-4 (trade)
    ISBN 0-8094-6513-2 (library)
    1. Earth—Religious aspects.   2. Nature—Religious
aspects.
I. Time-Life Books.   II. Series.
BL438.2.E27 1991
130—dc20   90-20666
                                                       CIP

MYSTERIES OF THE UNKNOWN

SERIES EDITOR: Jim Hicks
Series Administrator: Jane A. Martin
Art Director: Herbert H. Quarmby
Picture Editor: Susan V. Kelly

Editorial Staff for *Earth Energies*
Text Editors: Robert A. Doyle (principal), Janet Cave
Senior Writers: Esther R. Ferington, Margery A. duMond
Associate Editor/Research: Christian D. Kinney
Assistant Editors/Research: Constance Contreras, Denise
Dersin (lead research)
Assistant Art Director: Susan M. Gibas
Writer: Marfé Ferguson Delano
Copy Coordinators: Colette Stockum (principal), Donna
Carey
Picture Coordinator: Michael Kentoff
Editorial Assistant: Donna Fountain

Special Contributors: Carol A. Diuguid, Sheila M. Green,
Patricia A. Paterno, Susan Perry, Evelyn S. Prettyman,
Nancy J. Seeger (research); John Clausen, Norman S.
Draper, Douglas C. Logan, Harvey S. Loomis, John I. Mer-
ritt, Jake Page, Curtis W. Prendergast, Robert H. White
(text); John Drummond (design); Hazel Blumberg-McKee
(index).

Correspondents: Elisabeth Kraemer-Singh (Bonn), Christine
Hinze (London), Christina Lieberman (New York), Maria
Vincenza Aloisi (Paris), Ann Natanson (Rome).
Valuable assistance was also provided by Mehmet Ali
Kislali (Ankara); Angelika Lemmer (Bonn); Bing Wong
(Hong Kong); Judy Aspinall, Lesley Coleman (London);
Meenakshi Ganguly, Deepak Puri (New Delhi); Elizabeth
Brown (New York); Ann Wise (Rome); Mieko Ikeda, Win-
ston Priest (Tokyo).

Consultants:
Marcello Truzzi, general consultant for the series, is a
professor of sociology at Eastern Michigan University. He
is also director of the Center for Scientific Anomalies
Research (CSAR) and editor of its journal, the *Zetetic
Scholar*. Dr. Truzzi, who considers himself a "constructive
skeptic" with regard to claims of the paranormal, works
through the CSAR to produce dialogues between critics
and proponents of unusual scientific claims.

John Allee, an authority on Taoist traditions, is a teacher
of Chinese philosophy and medicine. He is on the faculty
of the Oregon College of Oriental Medicine and lectures at
Portland State University. Dr. Allee is currently writing a
book on Chinese approaches to longevity.

Other Publications:

TIME-LIFE LIBRARY OF CURIOUS AND UNUSUAL FACTS
AMERICAN COUNTRY
THE THIRD REICH
VOYAGE THROUGH THE UNIVERSE
THE TIME-LIFE GARDENER'S GUIDE
TIME FRAME
FIX IT YOURSELF
FITNESS, HEALTH & NUTRITION
SUCCESSFUL PARENTING
HEALTHY HOME COOKING
UNDERSTANDING COMPUTERS
LIBRARY OF NATIONS
THE ENCHANTED WORLD
THE KODAK LIBRARY OF CREATIVE PHOTOGRAPHY
GREAT MEALS IN MINUTES
THE CIVIL WAR
PLANET EARTH
COLLECTOR'S LIBRARY OF THE CIVIL WAR
THE EPIC OF FLIGHT
THE GOOD COOK
WORLD WAR II
HOME REPAIR AND IMPROVEMENT
THE OLD WEST

*For information on and a full description of any of the Time-
Life Books series listed above, please call 1-800-621-7026 or
write:*
Reader Information
Time-Life Customer Service
P.O. Box C-32068
Richmond, Virginia 23261-2068

This volume is one of a series that examines the history
and nature of seemingly paranormal phenomena. Other
books in the series include: